Douglas Barnes

From Communication to Curriculum

Second Edition

With an Afterword by Kathryn Mitchell Pierce

D1264551

Boynton/Cook Publishers
Heinemann
Portsmouth, NH

BOYNTON/COOK PUBLISHERS, INC.
A subsidiary of
HEINEMANN EDUCATIONAL BOOKS, INC.
361 Hanover Street   Portsmouth, NH 03801
Offices and agents throughout the world

First edition published 1976 by Penguin Books, London.
Second edition published 1992 by Boynton/Cook–Heinemann, Portsmouth, New Hampshire.

Acknowledgements
I am grateful to Mrs. Mary Walsh and to Oxford University Press for permission to reproduce the poem 'The Bully Asleep' from The *Roundabout by the Sea* by the late John H. Walsh and to J.M. Dent and Sons, and Jenny Joseph for permission to reproduce the poem 'Warning' by Jenny Joseph from *Rose in the Afternoon*.

Library of Congress Cataloging-in-Publication Data
Barnes, Douglas R.
      From communication to curriculum / Douglas Barnes : with an
afterword by Kathryn Mitchell Pierce. — 2nd ed.
          p.   cm.
      Includes bibliographical references and index.
      ISBN 0-86709-298-X
      1. Teacher-student relationships.   2. Communication in education.
3. Group work in education.   I. Title
LB1033.B36   1992
371.1'023 — dc20   91-31736
                                                        CIP

Front-cover design by Max-Karl Winkler.

Printed in the United States of America.
92 93 94 95 96 9 8 7 6 5 4 3 2 1

Contents

Preface to the Second Edition

It is a pleasure to introduce to new readers a book that has for some years influenced teachers in the United Kingdom and Australia but has not been easily available in North America. Teachers on both sides of the Atlantic now understand more clearly how important it is for their students to be actively engaged in the task of learning. Learning is not just a matter of receiving information; students need to be helped to develop their grasp of new ideas and ways of understanding and to relate them to their existing experience of the world. When I wrote this book I wanted to show how children when they talk and write can be "working on understanding". The teacher's role in setting up opportunities for students to do this is crucial, for it is all too easy to discourage them, or trap them in the routine reproduction of unassimilated information.

This book is addressed to all teachers, whatever subjects they teach and whatever the ages of their students. The examples of students' talk are taken from a wide range of curriculum subjects, including the sciences, history, geography, and English, and could well have included mathematical and technical subjects too, since all should involve investigating, planning, trying out, reflecting, and evaluating. Most of the students in the examples are eleven to thirteen years of age, like those to be found in elementary, middle, or junior high schools in the United States or Canada. (The U.K. system is different, in that many secondary schools receive their students at eleven or twelve years of age.) However, teachers in the United States have already shown that much younger children, even in kindergarten and first grade, can engage in useful learning talk in small groups if the topic is well chosen and they have been carefully shown what is expected of them. One group of such teachers (in St. Louis) is led by Kathryn Mitchell Pierce, who has contributed an Afterword to this edition, in which she explains what these ideas have meant to her and to the teachers she has worked with.

If the major focus of education in the eighties was the development of more sophisticated approaches to the teaching of writing via the examples of such writers as Donald Graves and Lucy Calkins, there are clear signs that the nineties will focus upon "whole language" approaches. The central assumption of the whole language movement is that children's language, including their literacy skills, develops as a whole, through talking, reading, and writing that relate to their own current interests and understanding. This book develops in detail several aspects of a whole language approach to the curriculum.

Central to the book is the idea of "exploratory talk", students working in small groups to make connections, re-arrange, reconceptualise, and internalise the new experiences, ideas, and ways of knowing offered in the curriculum. Teachers need to understand how to set up, develop, and support this kind of talking for learning. Small group talk, however, can never constitute more than part of the complex activities of the classroom, so that attention must also be given to other exchanges between teacher and taught. Thus a second concern is to show how teachers, in setting up and participating in learning activities, influence for good or ill the kinds of participation in learning what will be open to their students.

The call to go "back to basics", which seems always to be with us in one form or another, is based upon a misleading view of how learning takes place. Teaching is not just a matter of presenting to students "bite-sized chunks" of information or skill. Constructivist theorists tell us that unless the students are making sense for themselves of the experiences made available in the curriculum, trying out the ideas and skills, making links with their previous experience, looking for positive or discomforting examples, applying ideas to new contexts, and so on — then they will quickly forget what has been offered to them. All teachers need to be able to argue against reductive pictures of what constitutes teaching and learning.

Many teachers, like those in St. Louis, have found it useful to tape-record their students in order to find out how talking contributes to learning, for through close analysis of what is said they can see how their students are able to transmute what they have been taught and make it their own. Moreover, even quite young children display in exploratory talk impressive interpersonal skills that are often invisible in conventional classes. Some of the bravest teachers have gone on to investigate their own contributions to lessons and how these shape students' talking and writings. Such investigation and reflection by practising teachers is worth many pages of formal research carried out by others, for this helps them to become better listeners to their students, more aware both of the importance of talk in learning and of their own influence upon it.

Douglas Barnes

Leeds, June 1991

Preface to the First Edition

In this book I have set out to illustrate some ways in which children use speech in the course of learning, and to indicate how this depends upon the patterns of communication set up by teachers in their classrooms. In one direction this leads towards the practical: there is a great need for all teachers to understand how their communicative behaviour influences their pupils' learning. At the same time, however, I have been concerned with the curriculum and with appropriate ways of discussing it. Orthodox curriculum theory derives its analysis of curriculum process from the teacher's objectives; I have argued here that, since the learner's understandings are the *raison d'être* of schooling, an adequate curriculum theory must utilize an interactive model of teaching and learning. Thus this discussion of communication is intended – over and above its practical relevance – to be a critical contribution to curriculum theory.

A preface is a proper place for acknowledging debts, though my first two debts are far too long-standing to apply to this book alone. For twenty years I have benefitted from James Britton's delicate and responsible thinking about education; I can only hope that he will approve this superstructure which I have erected. I am glad also to be able to acknowledge my considerable debt, both here and in earlier papers on classroom communication, to Harold Rosen: I have learnt a great deal from his conversation and his writings. We owe much to a critic who can face us with those counter-arguments which were before no more than uneasiness at the periphery of vision.

To Frankie Todd I am indebted not only for criticism of an earlier draft of this book but also for the education which comes from collaborating across the divide of different academic backgrounds. For some years John Dixon and I have shared an interest in the analysis of small-group talk, and I have benefited both from his ideas and from his encouragement. I owe thanks to Frank Dawson and to Peter Davies for permission to quote from materials collected by each of them, to Denis Shemilt for the very substantial part he played in the study of Transmission and Interpretation described in Chapter Five, to Mrs Muriel Pyrah for permission to quote from a lesson, to Mrs Connie Langton for typing from my manuscript, and to many of my students in the University of Leeds Institute of Education. I owe particular thanks to Mr T. G. B. Howe, headmaster of John Smeaton School, Leeds, and to his colleagues and pupils. They have been most helpful, not only in allowing me to tape-record small-group discussions, but also in making positive contributions to the planning and interpreting of the recordings.

A completed book, printed and bound, seems to lay claim to a finality which contradicts the author's memories of indecision when he sat, pen in hand, struggling to give form to his intentions. If this book seems in this or that turn of phrase to make dogmatic claims, the reader is asked to discount them as he reads. The author is well aware of the slender evidence on which some of his assertions rest, and wishes the book to be read as a hypothetical contribution to an infant line of thought which will undoubtedly undergo radical development.

Douglas Barnes

Leeds, September 1974

Chapter One
Two Aspects of Classroom Language

1. Talking in Class

Schools are places where people talk to one another. And where they write for one another. Nothing could be more obvious. But is it as straightforward as that? Isn't most of the writing done by the younger persons present? There is usually an older person called a 'teacher' present in the room where young 'pupils' are writing: does he also write? We certainly see these teachers writing with chalk on certain walls though they seem annoyed when their pupils write with chalk on other walls. What they write also seems to be rather different. The teachers also make red marks on the papers which their pupils give them. Although the children do pieces of writing to give to the teachers, we do not seem to find many teachers doing pieces of writing for the children. There seems to be some agreement about who writes where, in what way and about what subject-matter and for whose eyes. Sometimes the teacher seems to enforce the arrangement, but for the most part it is tacitly agreed. For example, we do not see any children making marks in red ink on other people's writing.

Perhaps there are also agreements about who talks to whom, and when and how. We eavesdrop on one lesson and notice that although there is only one adult in the room, she seems to be talking more than all the children together. She is the centre of everybody's attention: she asks many questions, and demands answers as of right. 'What other ways are there of measuring it?' she asks, and goes on urgently, 'Come on. More hands up. Have you all gone to sleep?' In spite of this urgency she seems to know the answer already, for she dismisses several suggestions until one comes which she greets with, 'That's it. Good answer, John.' Her young pupils ask hardly any questions, except for permission to fetch ink from the cupboard. When one or two children shout answers without first being named by her, she checks them with a cryptic 'Hands?' which they seem to understand as a reproof. Only one child changes the subject of the conversation; he tells an anecdote about his dog, to which the teacher listens politely but with some signs of impatience. No child asks questions like those the teacher asks; no pupil says: 'What is normally awarded for an unfair charge outside the penalty area?' or continues, 'Really, Mrs Jones, I would have thought that by your age you would know something as obvious as that.'

If we look in at Mrs Jones's class tomorrow we may see a different pattern of behaviour. Perhaps every child will be writing or drawing, while Mrs Jones walks round engaging individuals in conversation about their work. Every now and again she indicates by an accusing look or word that silence is expected, but in fact she tolerates a good deal of surreptitious conversation – a strange contradiction between explicit demands and behaviour which pupils and teacher alike covertly accept. On another occasion a child tells the class about something she has done, until her hearers' interest wanes, and Mrs Jones steps in with a firm voice to command attention. Occasionally the class works in groups, perhaps with apparatus, or in preparing a group presentation of some kind. Then the room is full of noise, and from time to time Mrs Jones uneasily hushes the children, particularly if someone passes in the corridor. But time and time again Mrs Jones and her class return to the pattern of communication in which we first saw them, when Mrs Jones uses her voice to control and shape the thoughts and attention of the class.

Of course, we all 'know' why the children and the teacher are there in the classroom. We know because we have learnt about schooling by taking part in the game. We have all learnt to play in the 'pupil' position. Many of the readers of this book will have played in the 'teacher' position too. For us this has become invisible knowledge, invisible because we take it for granted. It is hard to recover invisible knowledge and see it afresh: how would we perceive a classroom if we had never seen it before? All we can do is to play the anthropologist. We can pretend to look through ignorant eyes and ask questions about what Mrs Jones says to her pupils, and why they respond as they do. But to frame the questions and answer them we must grope towards our invisible knowledge and bring it into sight. Only in this way can we see the classroom with an outsider's eye but an insider's knowledge, by seeing it as if it were the behaviour of people from an alien culture. Then by an act of imagination we can both understand better what happens and conceive of alternative possibilities.

Here are some of the questions that we can ask. Who has decided that the patterns of talk and writing are as they are? Who decides what constitutes 'shouting out' or 'untidy work'? How do these patterns change? How do children – or teachers – learn them? How much of what goes on contributes to children's learning and how much performs other functions? What are these functions? And are these different from the purposes which teachers and pupils believe them to be serving? Does their behaviour always match their conscious intentions? What in fact is the connection between the teacher's intentions and the day-by-day life in the classroom?

Every classroom has its ways of going about things. Although teachers do not like to be told so, these are surprisingly consistent from one classroom to another. They include, as I have suggested, very complex patterns of expectation about who says what to whom and when. But they also include ways of making sense of what happens and these are not by any means static. The meanings available in the classroom are open to perpetual renewal and change: for this reason there are dangers in the metaphor which I have been using of classroom learning as a game with rules to be learnt. This may describe some classrooms where teacher and tradition determine the rules and the children have to learn them before they can join in the game. But it is a very different kind of game in other classrooms, where there may be areas bounded by rules but other areas where the rules themselves are open to change. It is not easy to think of a game in which the point lies in changing the rules as you play it, so here the metaphor loses its value. I mean that children are not merely passive recipients; in many classrooms they learn ways of making new meanings.

Of course, it is not only in classrooms that people talk to one another. Outside in the street, in shops and buses, in offices and on building-sites, people are constantly talking. No doubt we could frame rules for what a shopkeeper can say to his customers without going beyond 'shopkeeper' and becoming 'fellow human being'. Even these temporary relationships are potentially infinite, capable of developing new common meanings as acquaintanceship becomes friendship and so on. In one way schools are different, because unlike shop, bus and building-site *they are there purely for the talk*. A school in its very nature is a place where communication goes on: that is what it is for. Education is a form of communication. (I must hastily ask you not to translate this into, 'All teachers have to do is to tell their pupils what they need to know'.)

When people talk about 'the school curriculum' they often mean 'what teachers plan in advance for their pupils to learn'. But a curriculum made only of teachers' intentions would be an insubstantial thing from which nobody would learn much. To become meaningful a curriculum has to be enacted by pupils as well as teachers, all of whom have their private lives outside school. By 'enact' I mean come together in a meaningful communication – talk, write, read books, collaborate, become angry with one another, learn what to say and do, and how to interpret what others say and do. A curriculum as soon as it becomes more than intentions is embodied in the communicative life of an institution, the talk and gestures by which pupils and teachers exchange meanings even when they quarrel or cannot agree. In this sense curriculum is a form of communication.

When I described some of the patterns of communication set up by Mrs Jones in different lessons, I was not just presenting these as different social relationships but as part of what her pupils were learning. We cannot make a clear distinction between the content and the form of the curriculum, or treat the subject-matter as the end and the communication as no more than a means. The two are inseparable. Let us take as an example a range of different ways of teaching the 'same' content, perhaps the way of life of urban working people at the beginning of the nineteenth century. One teacher may talk to a class about this, and then ask questions to elicit the same material from her pupils. Another teacher may first issue a folder of facsimiles, pictures, and other evidence from the period and then ask the pupils to build up a written account. Or, using the same folder, another may set a problem to pupils: 'Were people satisfied with their way of life?' and set children to work in small groups identifying evidence pro and contra. The teacher may ask pupils to report orally on what they have found, or to prepare a wall display, or to write an account purely for her eyes. When she leads discussion of what they have found out, she may guide them along a closely predetermined route, or follow ideas raised by pupils. In all of these cases the topic remains in some sense the same; it is the communication that differs. As the form of communication changes, so will the form of what is learnt. One kind of communication will encourage the memorizing of details, another will encourage pupils to reason about the evidence, and a third will head them towards the imaginative reconstruction of a way of life. From the communication they will also learn what is expected of them as pupils, how sharply Mrs Jones will apply her own criteria of relevance, whether they are expected to have ideas of their own or only to remember what they have been told. That is, they will find out how far they are expected to take part in the formulating of knowledge, or whether they are to act mainly as receivers.

I have already indicated in my description of Mrs Jones's imaginary lesson something of what constitutes the communication system of a classroom. Another way of approaching this would be to ask what small children have to learn in order to become part of the normal life of a school. Robert Dreeben[1] has argued that they have to learn (1) to be independent (2) to accept treatment as a member of a class rather than as a unique person (3) to compete with one another. Philip Jackson[2] on the other hand emphasizes *crowds*, *praise*, and *power*. Children have to learn to inhibit their impulses, to wait their turn, avoid physical

1. Dreeben, R. (1967), 'The Contribution of Schooling to the Learning of Norms', *Harvard Educational Review* 37:2.
2. Jackson, P. W. (1968), *Life in Classrooms*, Holt, Rinehart & Winston.

aggression, accept the teacher's authority, and guide their behaviour by her evaluation.

These are large-scale matters, however, which seem to miss
many of the details which I pointed out in Mrs Jones's lesson.
Children have to learn what kinds of things teachers say and do,
and what they expect their pupils to say and do in reply. They
have a good deal of elbow-room but not an infinite amount – as
I hinted in my imaginary example of a pupil using red ink on a
teacher's work, or evaluating her reply to a question about foot-
ball. Even the most rebellious children don't do things quite like
that.

Children have to learn how to interpret teachers' remarks. A
teacher once asked a pupil to read aloud, but after he had read
a sentence or two she interrupted him with, 'Begin again, John.
No one can hear you.' Another pupil, interpreting this literally,
told the teacher that he *could* hear, much to the teacher's surprise.
The teacher's statement 'No one can hear you' was effectively
an injunction to John to project his voice. The other pupil failed
to understand this, and replied to it as if it were a descriptive
statement, as its form would suggest. But this is perhaps to overemphasize the learning of classroom signals, for we undertake
similar learning whenever we take on a new job or join a new
club.

Other kinds of social learning may have greater importance:
consider how the pattern of a teacher's questions tends to signal
to pupils whether they are expected, for example, to think aloud
or to supply a 'right answer', whether they should obey an implicit command or merely show understanding of a statement.
Add to this the great power of the teacher's reply. This includes
not only the explicit evaluation – 'Splendid, Mary, that's just
what I wanted' – but also the unenthusiastic 'Yes' or 'Well I
suppose so . . . but I was thinking . . .' Most teacher-class discussions that go on day after day in schools are shaping not only
pupils' thinking but their behaviour as learners too. Of course,
some teachers control what goes on in their lessons less tightly
than others do, so that pupils can take a larger part in the shaping
of meaning, in the enacting of the curriculum.

And teachers have stronger sanctions. We may hear the threatening tones of 'I can see what you're doing, John Jones, and I won't have it'. At its most extreme speech becomes a weapon, asserting the finality of a teacher's control over a pupil. There is no need to add more examples; anyone who has attended a school knows how the communication system indicates to pupils the boundaries of who they are and what they may do.

This kind of social learning has recently been much discussed under the name of the 'implicit' or 'hidden curriculum'. It is curriculum in the sense that it is undoubtedly part of what pupils have to learn in school. Just as much part of curriculum as textbooks, learning apparatus or syllabus content, it is often learnt more successfully. It contrasts with the manifest curriculum in that few teachers deliberately plan to teach it, and many are even unaware of its existence. They therefore take no responsibility for these social demands which the school makes upon pupils. Teachers should be more aware of and should take responsibility for the hidden curriculum.

But the idea of 'the hidden curriculum' gives a very one-sided view of what happens. In fact, pupils are never passive recipients of social conditioning. Even in the most authoritarian school there are pupils who find opportunities to elude the pressure to conform; as Hargreaves[3] has shown, there may even be tacit agreements between teachers and pupils to subvert the expectations which all pay lip-service to. It is surprising how seldom pupils operate the veto which they have in their power. In most schools the social surface is preserved intact by teachers and pupils alike. The power which pupils do often operate is that of opting out; they conform, and even play the system, but many do not allow the knowledge presented to them to make any deep impact upon their view of reality.

The hidden curriculum is as much part of curriculum as is the manifest curriculum which is set out in syllabuses and textbooks. In order to join in the life of the school each child *must* learn to adopt the expected behaviour. It is both pervasive and imperceptible, unless we set ourselves to perceive it. You may have noticed that I have moved from the communication system of the class-

3. Hargreaves, D. H. (1967), *Social Relations in a Secondary School*, Routledge & Kegan Paul.

room to the communication system of the school. These are not identical: a teacher can often set up an incompatible system within the walls of his classroom stronghold. But if he does there are likely to be considerable pressures brought to bear upon him; there is a hidden curriculum for teachers too.

2. From Communication to Learning

Nearly everything which I have said so far treats pupils as passive receivers of training and socialization. But this is only one side of education. What does the learner himself contribute? This is partly a matter of the knowledge which he brings to school from his life outside it. What part do the learner's purposes, interests, values play in his schooling? It is not only teachers who have 'objectives'. We can also ask what the learner does in order to learn, for learning is not just a matter of sitting there waiting to be taught. If we think of what goes on in schools solely in terms of conformity to norms, we omit the school's manifest purpose, the pupils' participation in the enactment of knowledge. When we look at the communication system of a school or classroom we can ask: What part do the learners play in the formulation of knowledge? Where does speech come in this?

As infants we learn to speak as part of learning to be a member of the family. Learning to join in the meanings which are shared by the family in day-to-day communication is identical with becoming a member of the family. Of course, this communication is not just a matter of language. As the child grows older, however, he begins to use for new purposes the speech which he learnt for communication, talking aloud to himself as he plays with his toys. At first he uses this 'egocentric speech' just as an accompaniment to his play, telling himself what he is doing. Later (as Vygotsky pointed out) he will learn to use speech to plan what he is going to do, or to recall and re-experience what has already happened, re-interpreting this incidentally while doing so

Eventually all children learn to use speech to make things up. We might hear a five-year-old who is playing with a row of boxes (which he calls a train) call out: 'We're coming to a station. There's the ticket man. Get your tickets out.' Here in embryo we have the use of language to transcend the here and now by constructing a new reality. From this will later come the ability not only to make up stories but also to set up hypotheses and form theories. Although I am stressing the part played by language, this view does not in the least conflict with Piaget's view that beyond speech and play alike lies a general human ability to symbolize reality to oneself and to others.

The child originally learnt speech for communication with others but is now using that speech for himself. Speech is now part of his own thinking and imagining, and not always used for communicating these to other people. Vygotsky argued for the existence of an 'inner speech' which for adults is the silent equivalent of children's egocentric speech. Such inner speech would be the most accessible part of thought, thus making our thinking and feeling open to introspection and control.

Certainly many adults report an audible inner monologue that comments, interprets and guides through much of their waking hours. Often when we meet a problem we want to talk it over; the phrase 'talk it over' seems to imply something other than communicating ideas already formed. It is as if the talking enabled us to rearrange the problem so that we can look at it differently. Such talking is as much for ourselves as for the other persons present. It is quite different from persuading someone to do what one wants and from negotiating consensus in a committee.

Thus we cannot consider language in the classroom only in terms of communication, but must consider how children themselves use language in learning. The major means by which children in our schools formulate knowledge and relate it to their own purposes and view of the world are speech and writing. This is not to ignore the knowledge which exists in manipulating abilities and skills, and in the perception and control of visual patterning. The importance of language – and of other symbolic systems such as mathematics – is that it makes knowledge and thought processes readily available to introspection and revision. If we know what we know, then we can change it. Language is not the same as thought, but it allows us to reflect upon our thoughts. The metaphor contained in 'reflect' is here highly appropriate: what we say and write mirrors our thought processes, and enables us to take responsibility for them. Thus children and adults alike are not only receiving knowledge but remaking it for themselves.

One purpose of this book is to explore the relationship between communication and learning in school. To put it this way may seem to imply that there is a thing 'curriculum' (or 'education') and an activity 'communication' which puts that curriculum into effect. I wish to argue to the contrary that curriculum should be treated as composed of meaningful activities; and that amongst these activities are those we call communication. Not only is talking and writing a major means by which people learn, but what they learn can often hardly be distinguished from the ability to communicate it. Learning to communicate is at the heart of education.

What pupils learn must be closely related to what they do, but 'do' here includes what interpretation they put upon their actions. The talk and writing that goes on in lessons is part of that interpretation, and thus intimately involved in what is learnt. If teachers understand the patterns of communication in their lessons they can take more responsibility for what their pupils learn.

3. Teaching and Learning

It is probable that to most adults, including many teachers, the statement 'Teachers communicate knowledge to their pupils' would seem an adequate account of how a curriculum is put into effect. One hears the phrases 'transmitting knowledge' and 'handing on the culture'. This is an inadequate and partial account which is therefore very misleading. Let us look more closely at what happens in a particular lesson.

A history teacher is telling a mixed-ability class of twelve-year-olds about life in the Middle Ages. Their books are open at a drawing of a medieval village and he has been telling them at length about each of the buildings in the drawing. Occasionally he addresses a question to a pupil, and on one occasion a question leads to a longer exchange:

T There's another building there, not a house but what?
P A mill.
T A mill, a mill. We have lots of mills around this area. This isn't the sort of mill we have around here. What goes on in this mill?
P Sir, water.
T Pardon.
Ps Water . . . for washing.
T Washing? [Laughter] . . . It's not a washing mill. Yes, D—.
P Is it a power house?
T A power house for what?
P Electricity.

What was happening in that lesson might at first glance have seemed to be the handing on of knowledge, but as soon as the pupils had the opportunity to engage in the formulating of knowledge it becomes clear that 'handing on' is an inadequate metaphor. The pupils are interpreting what the teacher says through what they already know: they have no other means of interpretation. Thus the mill because it is associated with water must either be for washing raw wool, or for producing electricity.

What has happened is clear enough from the teacher's point of view. He has explained life in a medieval village; most pupils have listened, and one or two misunderstood about the mill in an amusing way. All is normal. Pupils and teacher know the rules of the game and play it accordingly. But this is only the surface of what is happening. The 'misunderstandings' are not merely an amusing lapse but a normal part of learning. While the teacher goes on talking we cannot tell what his pupils are making of what he says, but we can be sure that each of them is interpreting it in terms of what he already knows. This only becomes obvious, though, when they are able to join in.

What will the pupils take away with them? It will certainly be different from what the teacher believes himself to be teaching. Every pupil in the class will go away with a version of the lesson, which in some respects is different from all of the other pupils' versions, *because what each pupil brings to the lesson will be different*. Thus we shall not be able to understand what they learn without considering that they make sense of new knowledge by projecting it upon what they know already. Classroom learning can be best seen as an interaction between the teacher's meanings, and those of his pupils, so that what they take away is partly shared and partly unique to each of them.

What I am implying of course is the familiar idea that children are not 'little vessels . . . ready to have imperial gallons of facts poured into them until they were full to the brim', as Dickens put it. They have a personal history outside the school and its curriculum. In order to arrive at school they have mastered many complex systems of knowledge: otherwise they could not cope with everyday life. School for every child is a confrontation between what he 'knows' already and what the school offers; this is true both of social learning and of the kinds of learning which constitute the manifest curriculum. Whenever school learning has gone beyond meaningless rote, we can take it that a child has made some kind of relationship between what he knows already and what the school has presented.

It is misleading to see learning as the adding of new blocks of knowledge to an existing pile of blocks. Cognitive psychologists such as Piaget and Bruner have given us the metaphor of knowledge as series of systems for interpreting the world. From this point of view learning is a matter of changing the system by which interpretation is carried out. When children see an air-pump attached to a metal can, which then collapses, their very perception of this is an act of interpretation. They can only grasp the pattern of events which they are witnessing by interpreting them through analogous patterns which they are familiar with – the behaviour of balloons, bicycle tyres and so on. Indeed, all of our perception of reality – our 'knowledge' – can be explained as the operations of interpretative schemes upon the data presented to our eyes and other senses. As the events happen we tend to squeeze them to fit our interpretative categories. Piaget calls this 'assimilation'. At the same time, however, we modify our expectations to make them explain the events more adequately, and this complementary process Piaget calls 'accommodation'. By the simultaneous action of assimilation and accommodation the events are perceived as meaningful *and at the same time* generate changes in the interpretative procedures. These changes are transformations not additions. As a result, further examples of the operation of reduced air pressure will be interpreted by explanatory procedures which have assimilated the example of the can which collapsed. This is what I meant by saying that we can treat learning as equivalent to changing the interpretative system by which events are perceived.

G. A. Kelly well expresses this view:

The universe is open to piecemeal interpretation. Different men construe it in different ways. Since it owes no prior allegiance to any one man's construction system, it is always open to reconstruction. Some of the alternative ways of construing are better adapted to man's purposes than others. Thus, man comes to understand his world through an infinite series of successive approximations. Life is characterized by the capacity of the living thing to represent its environment. Especially is this true of man, who builds construction systems through which to view the real world.[4]

Kelly's formulation 'Man comes to understand his world through an infinite series of successive approximations' is interestingly similar to Piaget's statement: 'Knowledge . . . is a series of transformations that become progressively adequate.'[5] (I turn aside from the tempting question: 'Adequate to what?')

For older children and adults these transformations can be carried out not only in response to new sense data but also by communication with other people. I write 'communication' because I want to refer not only to verbal exchanges, but also to diagrams and pictures and to mathematic and logical symbols. It is as if we bring our own interpretative systems into interaction with the interpretative systems of other people; this is what is intended to happen when teacher and class discuss the collapsing can. It is all too possible for a teacher to be so intent on his own interpretation that it never comes into significant relationship to those of his pupils.

4. I owe this reference to Kelly, G. A. (1963), *A Theory of Personality* to James Britton, who discusses Kelly's views at length in his book *Language and Learning*, Penguin (1970).

5. Piaget, J. (1960), *Genetic Epistemology* Columbia University Press.

Our interpretative systems are modified not only by existential events and by communication with other people but by ourselves. Jerome Bruner writes: 'I suspect that much of growth starts out by our turning around and recoding in new forms ... what we have been doing or seeing, then going on to new modes of organization with the new products that have been formed by these recodings.'[6] The systems by which we 'organize' or interpret experience can be changed not only by new experiences but by representing old experiences to ourselves anew, and thus 're-coding' them in different forms. As James Britton puts it: 'Once we see man as creating a representation of his world so that he may operate in it, another order of activity is also open to him: he may *operate directly upon the representation itself.*'[7] Such representation must depend on a symbol system, either natural language or some other. This operating upon the representation is what I have called 'reflection'.

The idea of changing knowledge by recoding it, by verbalizing or in some other way, is so central to the argument of this book that I cannot overemphasize it. However, in quoting Bruner above I omitted a phrase and substituted the usual dots. What Bruner wrote was in fact: 'recoding in new forms *with the aid of an adult tutor*' (my italics). I omitted the latter part of the phrase not because I underestimate the importance of an auditor, but because Bruner's formulation closes several options which I wish to leave open to discussion. For example, can such recoding take place when the auditor is not an adult and when he is not a tutor? I hope to demonstrate that it can. Furthermore, can recoding (in Bruner's sense) take place when there is no auditor present, when the speaker is either talking to himself or to an imagined audience? Almost all writing is of this kind, for the writer is separated from the immediate promptings of an interlocutor. Does this mean that we cannot in writing make new meanings for ourselves? The part played by other people in the recoding of knowledge will be an important theme of this book.

6. Bruner, J. S. (1966), *Toward a Theory of Instruction*, Belknap Press, Harvard.
7. Britton, J. N. (1970), *Language and Learning*, Penguin.

4. Learning by Talking

It is now time to illustrate what I mean by 'Learning by Talking'. I shall do so by discussing a group of children making sense of a poem by talking their way into it. The example comes from English, but learning by talking can go on in History, Geography, Science, Mathematics, Religious Education indeed in any subject in which pupils can be presented with a problem which they are to solve by talking it over until they see possible solutions. I choose this discussion of a poem because it illustrates well certain aspects of learning by talking which would still apply if the pupils had been talking about different subject-matter.

The children are four eleven-year-old girls in their last term at a small primary school. The well-kept terrace houses round the school suggest that most of the children who attend the school are from good working-class homes. I tape-recorded all of the girls from the top class in four groups of four, talking about two poems which I had presented to them. I played to each group a recorded reading of the poem, gave each child a copy, and left them alone, saying 'Talk about the poems in any way you like, and let me know when you've finished.' All four groups talked for ten minutes or more, and grappled seriously with the task of understanding the poems. I shall select one short episode from one group's discussion, because it displays in a brief space several characteristics which are more diffusely present in all of the discussions.

The two poems which they read came from a volume called *The Roundabout by the Sea* by J. H. Walsh. It will be necessary to show you only one of the two poems, since the other is hardly mentioned in this discussion.

THE BULLY ASLEEP

One afternoon, when grassy
Scents through the classroom crept,
Bill Craddock laid his head
Down on his desk, and slept.

The children came round him:
Jimmy, Roger, and Jane;
They lifted his head timidly
And let it sink again.

'Look, he's gone sound asleep, Miss,'
Said Jimmy Adair;
'He stays up all the night, you see;
His mother doesn't care.'

'Stand away from him, children.'
Miss Andrews stooped to see.
'Yes, he's asleep; go on
With your writing, and let him be.'

'Now's a good chance!' whispered Jimmy;
And he snatched Bill's pen and hid it.
'Kick him under the desk hard;
He won't know who did it.'

'Fill all his pockets with rubbish –
Paper, apple-cores, chalk.'
So they plotted, while Jane
Sat wide-eyed at their talk.

Not caring, not hearing,
Bill Craddock he slept on;
Lips parted, eyes closed –
Their cruelty gone.

'Stick him with pins!' muttered Roger.
'Ink down his neck!' said Jim.
But Jane, tearful and foolish,
Wanted to comfort him.

When the following extract begins, the four girls have already been talking for several minutes. They have asked themselves whether a teacher would in real life have noticed that a boy had fallen asleep in a lesson.

1. Well the teacher's bound to notice.
2. Yes really ... because I mean ... I mean if ...
3. Or she could have gone out because someone had asked for her or something ... she probably felt really sorry for him so she just left him ... The teachers do ...

4. What really sorry for him . . . so she'd just left him so they could stick pins in him.
5. Oh no she probably . . . with the 'whispered' . . . said 'whispered' . . .
6. Yes.
7. Yes but here it says . . . um . . . [rustling paper] . . . oh 'Stand away from him, children. Miss Andrews stooped to see.'
8. Mm.
9. So you'd think that she would do more really.
10. Yes . . . you'd think she'd um . . . probably wake . . . if she would really felt sorry for . . . sorry for him she'd . . .
11. She'd wake him.
10. [cont.] . . . wake him.
12. Oh no! . . . No, she wouldn't send him home alone . . . because . . . nobody's . . .
13. His mother's bad.
14. Yes.
15. His mother would probably go out to work.
16. Yes he'd get no sleep at home if his mum was there.
17. Might have to . . . might have to turn out and work.
18. It might be . . . his mother's fault that really he's like this.
19. Oh it will be . . . It always is.
20. Look here it says um . . . 'His eyes are . . .' Where is it? 'His dark eyes cruel and somehow sad.'
21. I think that just puts it doesn't it?
22. Yes.
23. There's always something like that.
[Pause]
24. He's unhappy. [Whispered]

The four girls here are talking first about teachers, and then about the mothers of naughty children. Their speech seems interrupted and not always very explicit, yet they seem to understand one another. When 5 says, 'Oh no she probably . . . with the "whispered" . . . said "whispered" ', 7 seems to understand her because she retorts, 'Yes but here it says . . .' and so on. From an outsider's point of view the talk is not well-organized, yet by the end of the sequence they seem to have reached the main point of the poem, and appreciated its summing up in the line 'His dark eyes cruel and somehow sad'.

It is worth looking closely at this short discussion because it illustrates certain aspects of learning talk that are not always easy to identify. Although one child tends to lead this discussion, she is not 'telling' the others, nor is she asking questions to test their knowledge, as teachers do. The girls work out their interpretation in collaboration: one puts forward a view, another takes it up and modifies it, another finds evidence, and another sums it up. Group discussions are not always as neat as this, as every teacher knows, but it is by such collaboration that a group will achieve whatever success it does achieve.

Consider number 10: 'Yes . . . you'd think she'd um . . . probably wake . . . if she would really felt sorry for . . . sorry for him she'd . . . wake him.' You may feel that as communication this leaves some thing to be desired. But, as I have already said, communication is not the only function of language. The hesitations and changes of direction have a different function: we usually call it 'thinking aloud'. Talking her way into the problem is enabling this girl to monitor her own thought, and reshape it. Talk is here a means for controlling thinking. So if a teacher is too concerned for neat well-shaped utterances from pupils this may discourage the thinking aloud.

In this book I call this groping towards a meaning 'exploratory talk'. It is usually marked by frequent hesitations, rephrasings, false starts and changes of direction. I want to argue that it is very important whenever we want the learner to take an active part in learning, and to bring what he learns into interaction with that view of the world on which his actions are based. That is, such exploratory talk is one means by which the assimilation and accommodation of new knowledge to the old is carried out.

In this case you may have noticed that the exploratory talk is marked also by hypothetical expressions: 'she *could have* gone out', 'she *probably* felt', ' *You'd think* . . .', '*Might have* to . . .' It is as if the girls were perpetually reminding themselves and one another that they were only putting up a hypothetical explanation and that every statement was open to modification. It may be that the hypothetical mode makes exploratory talk more easy to sustain since it keeps possibilities open. But this is at present far from certain.

The strategy adopted by this group is first to set up hypothetical explanations: for example, 3 says 'she probably felt really sorry for him so she just left him'. This hypothesis is tested in two ways – against their own experience and against the words of the poem. 3 herself supports her interpretation by the general observation 'The teachers do'. (This possibly means that 3 has noticed that teachers are capable of sympathizing with their pupils.) 4 questions this by pointing out that leaving the boy asleep and vulnerable would be potentially unkind. They then turn to the text, and 5 points out the significant word 'whispered', significant, I think, because it indicates the teacher's solicitous desire to avoid waking the boy.

The absence of a teacher has placed control of learning strategies in the pupils' hands. In this case, since no task was set, the children control the questions that they choose to ask: the issue of whether the teacher acted wisely is theirs, not the poet's. But the teacher's absence removes from their work the usual source of authority; they cannot turn to him to solve dilemmas. Thus in this discussion – and in others which we shall come to later – the children not only formulate hypotheses, but are compelled to evaluate them for themselves. This they can do in only two ways: by testing them against their existing view of 'how things go in the world', and by going back to the 'evidence'. In this case the evidence is a poem, but it might equally have been a map, a facsimile of a historical document, a table of numerical data, or a piece of scientific apparatus.

My point here is not to recommend group work – though it has its value – but to consider the part played by speech in all this. The more a learner controls his own language strategies, and the more he is enabled to think aloud, the more he can take responsibility for formulating explanatory hypotheses and evaluating them. It is not easy to make this possible in a typical lesson: my contention at this point is that average pupils of secondary school age are capable of this if they are placed in a social context which supports it.

In this discussion the eleven-year-old girls are able to bring their everyday knowledge – of teachers and parents – to bear on a school task, and it is partly this that makes them seem more competent than we often expect eleven-year-olds to be. Many of the tasks set in schools do not make it easy for pupils to utilize their everyday knowledge. (I shall call this 'action knowledge' since it is the knowledge on which our actions in the everyday world are based.) Tasks may seem to relate to topics which they have never thought about before, or be couched in terms which give them no purchase on the problem, even when they do have action knowledge which is relevant. When the boundary between 'school knowledge' and 'action knowledge' is low and easy to cross, as in this discussion of *The Bully Asleep*, we can expect pupils to be able to take an active part in the formulation of knowledge. But it will only happen if the teacher allows for it, and sets up a communication system in which pupils have a considerable influence over moment-by-moment strategies – who asks what question, what evidence is treated as relevant, what counts as an acceptable answer, and so on.

These four girls show considerable competence not only in the content of what they say – making sense of the poem – but also in their social relationships. During their eleven years of life they have learnt a great deal about using language for collaborative thinking, for encouraging one another, for coping with disagreement, and for rational persuasion. If these skills, which are not unusual in eleven-year-olds, do not appear in lessons, this is partly because of the communication patterns of classroom and school.

In emphasizing children's use of language to participate in the shaping of knowledge I am of course making some assumptions about the kind of knowledge required. Talking will not necessarily contribute to recipe learning, the kind of learning in which the teacher wants the pupil to be able to feed back verbal formulae to him, without much care for underlying principles. When our purpose, however, is for pupils to grasp principles and to use the new knowledge as a means of recoding former experience, this kind of discussion seems of central importance. Much learning may go on while children manipulate science apparatus, or during a visit, or while they are struggling to persuade someone else to do what they want. But learning of this kind may never progress beyond manual skills accompanied by slippery intuitions unless the learners themselves have an opportunity to go back over such experience and represent it to themselves. There seems every reason for group practical work in science, for example, normally to be followed by discussion of the implications of what has been done and observed, since without this what has been half understood may soon slip away. Talk and writing provide means by which children are able to reflect upon the bases upon which they are interpreting reality, and thereby change them. Of course, this will not necessarily happen for every child in every conversation: discussions like the one about *The Bully Asleep* may be rare. It is for teachers to ask themselves how they can help pupils to achieve reflective talk and writing.

5. A Model of Communication and Learning

In the preceding sections I have presented language in two ways: first as a pattern of expectations which constitutes an important part of what children learn, and second as a means of learning, which they can use to make sense of what is presented to them, and relate it to what they already know. That is, I have distinguished speech as communication from speech as reflection. How are the two related to one another?

If a school's curriculum is taken to be those systems of meaning which are available to *and used by* teacher and pupil alike, what part is played in the collaborative construction of these meanings by speech and writing? Language must enter into the curriculum in two ways: (1) as the communication system of classroom and school; (2) as a means of learning. These two look at the same phenomena from two different directions. If we consider language solely as a communication system this could be taken to relegate the learner to a passive role as the recipient of socialization; if we consider language as a means of learning we regard the learner as an active participant in the making of meaning. This is no real contradiction, however. A communication system is an abstraction from the behaviour of a group of people; from one point of view it constrains them, but from another it exists only through what they do. The meanings that we live by change because we insensibly day by day renew them in the course of sharing our lives. The sharing is communication.

Since the social functions of language go on simultaneously with the making of meanings we have to consider how the two sets of functions interact. One would expect that the characteristics of each social context would limit the possibility of using language for the making of meanings. In an Anglican church service the congregation's part is limited to the acceptance of the common – and partly implicit – meanings enacted in the service: participation here means tacit acceptance. Members of the congregation are not expected to take an active part in the expression of new meanings.

Similarly, the expectations set up in a classroom, and more generally in a school, constrain – though in a greater or lesser degree – the pupils' participation in the shaping of learning. We can represent this as a diagram. The box at the left of the diagram

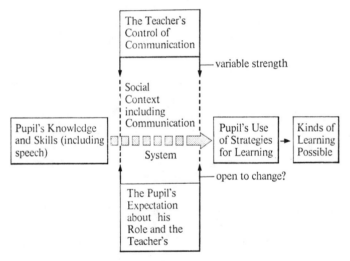

represents the learner's knowledge of English, which offers him a variety of ways of representing the world, and of strategies for solving problems. But his opportunity to put these into effect depends on the pattern of communication of that classroom, and this is represented by the central area of the diagram. The learning strategies which the pupils in fact use are filtered through this communication system, and this is symbolized by the heavy broken arrow. The communication system is a matter not only of how the teacher sets up classroom relationships and discourse (represented here by the downward-pointing arrows) but also of how the pupils interpret what the teacher does (represented here by the upward-pointing arrows). The communication pattern of any classroom is the outcome of a history of mutual interpretation by teacher and pupils, in each case based upon previous experiences which they bring to the lessons.

A child's participation in lessons does not arise solely from his individual characteristics – his 'intelligence', 'articulateness' or 'confidence' – but include the effects of his attempts to understand the teacher and the teacher's attempts to understand him. I have often noticed that teachers are willing to study their pupils' talk and other behaviour and yet leave themselves out of account, as if what they do and say has no effect upon the pupils. Similarly teachers often talk of pupils' behaviour as if it is *independent of what is being done to them*: '3c's in an awkward mood today.'[8] It is as if they delete from conscious awareness the part which they themselves play in classroom interaction. The purpose of the diagram is to make clear the part played by the teacher in shaping every pupil's participation in learning. Not only will he have set up in previous lessons some expectations about the kinds of behaviour he approves of, but in this very lesson his questions, his tone of voice, gestures and stance, the way he receives pupils' replies – the whole of his behaviour – will be affirming and re-affirming what uses of language he expects from pupils. So teacher and pupils join in setting up the social context or communication system, and it is this which will shape the range of language strategies used by pupils as they grapple with learning tasks.

In later chapters I shall illustrate some of the ways in which teachers set up norms for communication in their lessons, and how these affect their pupils' learning. This can then be related to teachers' beliefs about the nature of the knowledge which they are teaching. First, however, Chapter Two will be concerned with further examples of learning through group discussion.

---

8. I owe this latter point to Martin Hammersley (private communication).

Chapter Two
Learning in Small Groups

1. The Groups and their Tasks

In this chapter I abandon generalities for a while in order to look closely at four groups of twelve- to thirteen-year-old children talking while they are engaged in tasks set by their teachers. They were all members of the same second-year class in an unstreamed comprehensive school in the suburbs of a large city. I had asked their science teacher to choose four groups for me, two more and two less successful in science. Pupils in the school were not unaccustomed to working in small groups, since their teachers sometimes organized class-work in this way.

Group	Achievement in Science	Sex	Number
I	More successful	girls	3
II	More successful	boys	2
III	Less successful	girls	3
IV	Less successful	boys	3

So that I could compare how the groups used speech to grapple with different kinds of problem, I asked three of their teachers to plan with me a learning task in each of three subjects, Science, English and History. The recordings took place during appropriate lessons, and near the room in which the rest of the class was working. The pupils knew that they were being recorded by a visitor from the university.

Task	Subject	Materials	Place
1	Science	Apparatus and work cards	Curtained alcove off science laboratory
2	English	Copies and a recording of a poem	Partly enclosed work area
3	History	Labelled illustration in textbook	

The members of the four groups are listed below. No great weight should be placed on the estimates of IQ, which were drawn from group tests administered two years earlier under informal conditions. In the transcriptions each boy and girl will be referred to by an initial, but I have also given an imaginary name to each of them.

Group	Name	Symbol	IQ
I	Theresa	T	106
	Carol	C	Probably above average
	Betty	B	115
II	Glyn	G	117
	Steve	S	96
III	Frances	F	119
	Pauline	P	107
	Linda	L	86
IV	Richard	R	106
	John	J	101
	Anthony	A	91

Group II was made up of two boys only, chosen because they worked together particularly well in Science; on the last recording session one of them, Steve, was absent, and his place was taken by another boy. It should be noted that, since the groups were chosen by a teacher rather than by the pupils themselves, some of them may have had to face problems of personal relationships as well as the learning tasks set them.

The recordings on which this paper is based were made on three separate occasions. On each occasion each of the four groups was presented with a task or series of tasks:

1. *Air Pressure* The pupils were given written instructions to carry out a series of activities with physics apparatus which had been set up ready for them. This was not unlike the pattern of work in their normal physics lessons, except that on this occasion they were not asked to record results in writing. (This now seems an unfortunate omission.) The tasks included drinking milk through a straw, blowing between two apples suspended about an inch apart on long strings, and blowing into a stoppered jar in such a way that a small fountain resulted. In each case, pupils were asked to explain what they had observed.

2. *Warning* The pupils were presented with the poem *Warning* and told to talk about it in any way they wished. Each pupil was given a copy of the poem, and a recorded reading was played to each group before the discussion began.

3. *Saxon Settlement* Pupils were asked to imagine that they were Saxon invaders who were coming to settle in England, and to discuss what they would have to do and how they would do it. They were told that this was in preparation for individual pieces of writing on this topic. The class had given some time to the Saxon settlements during the previous term, and immediately before the discussions began they listened to a short talk and read a page from a book which also contained a sketch of a Saxon village.

In each case, after a group had indicated that they had completed their discussion, the teacher responsible for planning the activity joined them with the intention of asking what conclusions they had reached and of taking their discussion further. All of the discussions were recorded on tape, including those in which teachers participated, and have been transcribed. (Group I's discussion of the poem with the teacher was omitted because of a technical error.)

It was hoped that this study would throw light on these questions:

i. When pupils work in small groups what verbal strategies do they use in approaching various tasks? Which of these strategies prove more successful?

ii. Is the learning achieved by some groups limited by the range of verbal strategies available to them?

iii. What part is played by social pressures in learning? How far does interaction between pupils contribute to learning?

iv. How can small-group work be set up to achieve the best learning possible?

v. What should a teacher aim for when he joins in the discussion? What can he help a group to achieve that they are unlikely to achieve on their own? Can groups achieve anything alone which a teacher's presence inhibits?

These materials are not of a kind which would make a fully objective analysis fruitful. Not only is the sample too small, but the identification and description of learning strategies call for considerable exercise of judgement, the subjectivity of which must be acknowledged. I shall proceed by selecting passages from the transcriptions which are particularly productive in the sense that what the children say suggests that they are increasing their understanding. The learning strategies used in these passages will be discussed, and related to the particular context in which they have arisen. The overall purpose will be to arrive at some understanding of how pupils can use spoken language as a means of learning in various curricular subjects.

2. Air Pressure

I begin with the Science task. The following instructions were given in written form to each of the pupils.

AIR
In this work you are going to do some simple experiments about Air. Last term you studied Air, so you should not find them difficult! In each case do the work as it is described for you and then discuss amongst yourselves exactly what happened and why it happened. (Remember to give an explanation using the correct words.)

Experiment 1 Take a glass of milk and a transparent straw. Suck on the straw and drink some of the milk (not much – others have to do this work!).

Why is it you are able to drink in this way?

What actually happens?

Experiment 2 a. Get the two apples which are suspended from clamps. Put the apples within two inches of each other. Blow between the apples quite strongly and notice what happens.

b. Get two thin strips of paper and put them within one inch of each other. Again, blow between the strips. What happens?

Discuss amongst yourselves exactly what happens in each experiment. Is the idea the same in each case?

Experiment 3 Use the piece of apparatus like a bottle with a straw in the top. Rest it in a tray of some sort to collect any water. Blow into the 'straw' strongly for as long as you can. Stand back and watch what happens.

Discuss amongst yourselves exactly what you saw happening and try to give the best explanation you can.

It is difficult to make a sharp distinction between the verbal strategies adopted by the pupils in learning and the manner in which they negotiate relationships with one another. The success of a group appears to depend in part upon what might be called the level of interaction, that is, the extent to which members of the group are genuinely working together, trying to communicate and to understand.

Let us begin with the children's attempts to explain how it is possible to suck up milk through a straw. Group I begins:

5. T   It says, 'Why are you able to drink in this way?'
6. T   It's the suction . . . I think . . .
7.   Yer.
6. T [cont.] . . . that makes . . . that's why you can drink it.
8. T   Is that it?
9. C   Yer.

And there they leave the matter, never to return. They are very easily satisfied: Theresa finds a form of words and the others accept it without question. This is what I shall call a 'closed' approach to tasks: the group finds nothing to encourage active engagement, nothing to provoke questions or surmises. At this stage there is no evidence whether this closed approach is a general characteristic of this group, or whether it is partly provoked by this particular task. (Later Theresa treated similarly another of the teacher's instructions. She read aloud: 'Discuss among yourselves exactly what happened in each experiment. Is it the same idea in each one?' replied, 'Yes', and left it at that.)

Group III are no more successful in explaining the milk-drinking.

10. F   Because you're sucking air up, aren't you, from the . . .
11. ⎫
12. ⎭   Yes.
10. F [cont.] . . . from the little tube, that's why it comes up.
             [Pause]
13.   Hmm . . . what else?

Frances's use of the word 'sucking' is accepted as an adequate explanation, just as Theresa's 'suction' was. Both words seem to be providing the group with a pseudo-explanation, in order to enable them to move on to the next task. One wonders why the others do not challenge the words, asking for more explanation, and under what circumstances they would become aware that these explanations were inadequate. We might ask ourselves what constitutes an adequate explanation, and how we – or our pupils – know when we have achieved one. (For example, if we explain 'suction' in terms of 'air pressure', must we then explain 'air pressure'? And when do we stop?) How can they learn to be critical of their own explanations? The matter is not a simple one.

If we now move to the two boys of Group II we find at first an explanation which is only a little more satisfactory. Glyn says:

Why're you able to do this? Cos you make a vacuum with your . . . mouth, don't you? And then the water tries to fill the vacuum.

Then they move on to the next task. But Group II's approach to science is more 'open' in that they expect to find out something and therefore approach the task in a more flexible and inventive way. (It must be remembered that the difference between Groups I and II is not a simple matter of IQ.) It is particularly interesting that it is Steve, the 'less able' of the two, who suddenly – quite unprovoked and in the midst of a different discussion – calls them back to the first task.

(For the reader's convenience this dialogue and some others are presented with commentary beside them. It is intended that the dialogue be the first read through without the comments.)

Dialogue	Commentary
17. S What about what about this glass of milk though, Glyn?	Steve seems to have been uneasy about Glyn's previous explanation, as is indicated by his placing of the word 'though'.
18. G Well that's 'cause you make a vacuum in your mouth . . .	Glyn's answer to Steve's challenge is no more than a repetition of his previous vague account.
19. S When you drink the milk you see . . . you . . .	Steve seems dissatisfied, and sets off on a more explicit reply to his own question. When he hesitates he implicitly requires Glyn to complete the analysis by using the explanatory framework which he has set up.
20. G Right! . . . You you make a vacuum there, right?	Glyn's first 'Right' accepts the task. His second 'right' asks Steve whether his explanation so far is acceptable.
21. S Yes well you make a vacuum in the . . . er . . . transparent straw . . .	Steve does not find Glyn's use of 'there' explicit enough and (most usefully) insists that the vacuum is 'in the transparent straw'.
22. G Yes.	Glyn accepts the correction.
23. S Carry on.	Steve urges his friend to continue with the explanation.
24. G And the er air pressure outside forces it down, there's no pressure inside to force it back up again so . . .	Here Glyn achieves the essential explanatory point that it is the different pressures at the surface of the milk and inside the straw that make drinking possible.
25. S OK.	Steve accepts this version.

It is clear that Glyn would not have reached this level of explicitness in analysing the phenomena had it not been for the pressure which his friend puts upon him by questioning, by insisting upon explicit answers, and by setting up an explanatory framework. It is Steve who insists on 'in the transparent straw', and whose question helps Glyn to achieve the essential explanatory point that the pressure at the surface of the milk is greater than that within the straw. Thus the 'open' approach characteristic of this pair is largely due to the less able of them. More attention will later be given to questioning and to explicitness. The main point to be made here is that the social process contributed most importantly to the level of explanation reached: without Steve's help, Glyn would not have *represented to himself* so clearly what made drinking possible. They worked as partners in deliberately constructing a public statement which satisfied both as an adequate explanation. I am here making the central assumption that the shaping of language is a means by which pupils reach deeper understanding of what they have already partly grasped. To put it differently, not only did Steve learn from Glyn's explanation, but so did Glyn.

Compare this with part of Group III's discussion of the third task related to air pressure. This task required the pupils to blow into a stoppered flask through a tube which penetrated the stopper and ended below the surface of some water in the lower part of the jar. They were instructed to 'Blow into the "straw" strongly for as long as you can' and then to observe what happened. The air blown into the flask raised the pressure of the air above the water so that as soon as blowing ceased a jet of water was sent into the air. This surprised and delighted the girls of Group III, whose explanations so far had been as vague and unselfcritical as the one already quoted.

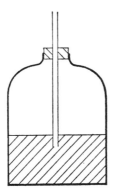

74. F	Perhaps all the water . . . that's come from the bubbles . . . goes up . . . goes up the tube and all that.
75. L	Look! It's coming out a' that . . . them little things there.
76.	It's 'cos it's got that . . . that stopper.
77.	Yes.
78.	You blow right hard and it . . . nothing happens.
79.	Nothing seems to happen.
80.	Let's have another go.
81.	Look! It's all coming out. Look! [Urgent]
81. [cont.]	. . . out of the straw.
83.	Yes.
84.	Ooh! Look at it all.
85.	What's next?
86. P	No, but how c . . . how can . . . er – how does it come up though? Look! It's still coming up.
88. F	Is it because of bubbles, because it blows bubbles?
89.	Yes . . . think so.
90. F	Or probably some gets up the straw and . . . 'cos look it's coming out of the top of the straw.

This passage has not been chosen as an example of Group III at their least successful; indeed, the dialogue – perhaps because of the unexpected shower of water – became more animated than before. (The girls' excitement has made it impossible to identify their voices with certainty.) Here they show a more 'open' engagement with the task than elsewhere in the 'air pressure' recordings. However, I quote this section in order to raise two questions: What signs are there here of potentially valuable learning strategies? In what way is it nevertheless unsatisfactory?

For the first time, one of the girls, Frances, spontaneously offers an explanatory suggestion (No. 74). Pauline (No. 86) asks the kind of question which had proved so useful to the boys of Group II: 'How does it come up though?' It fails to lead to a useful discussion because Frances's not very helpful answer, 'Is it because of bubbles?', is tamely accepted by the others. Similarly they accept the earlier attempt at explanation: 'Perhaps all the water . . . that's come from the bubbles . . . goes up the tube and all that.' This contrasts with Steve's and Glyn's urgent attentiveness to one another, and their insistence upon explicit statement. Group III girls, no less able than the boys, on the whole avoid challenging one another in these science tasks; they seem to work for the social smoothness of consensus. Nevertheless we should not underrate Pauline's question, which might in another context have proved valuable. There is a great deal of difference between the effect of questions asked by pupils of one another, and the effect of a teacher's questions, partly no doubt because the pupils are aware that the teacher usually 'knows the answer' already.

We shall not linger on this disappointing exchange, but will see how the girls of Group I approached this piece of apparatus.

35. T	[Reading] Blow into the ... Blow into the straw ... strongly for as long as you can. Stand back and watch what happens.
36. T	Ugh! ... The water comes up the straw. [Amused]
37. C	I wonder how that ... I wonder why ... How do you stop it?
38.	[Inaudible] ... it'll stop.
39. B	I wonder how it manages to do that. Right, you blow it ... right ... [Laughter] ... Pr – probably it's 'cos of the air pressure.
40. T	Yer ... it'll be the air pressure ... and [Clash of voices]
41. C	... it's the air pressure ...
42. C	It's pressing down on the water.
43. T	Yer, and it's coming up the tube.
44. B	Yer ... [Pause]
45. T	It's a good job I had that tray there.
46. T	[Reading] Discuss among yourselves exactly what you saw and try to give the best explanation you can.
47. C	Isn't it air pressure?
48. B	Air pressure yer ... when you blow ... it's, it's the
49. T	... it's the air pressure that's inside the tube.
48. B [cont.]	It's the air pressure ... when you blow down it presh ... er ... it presses on the ... water ... and it ... er ...
49. T [cont.]	Yer ... and it sends it 'em ... it sends it up and ...
48. B [cont.]	... it's the air that sends it up.

At first glance this seems almost as unsatisfactory as Group III's attempt. Notice the facile: 'It's 'cos of the air pressure' (No. 39) and the many occurrences of 'it' from No. 47 onwards.

No doubt these uses of 'it' are accompanied by gestures towards part of the apparatus; nevertheless, this must not hide from us that they have failed to make the process clear to themselves or to one another. In particular they fail to distinguish explicitly between the air pressure in the tube and that in the flask, a distinction which one might have thought within their reach. We should perhaps remind ourselves that Group II – who might equally well have pointed – made this distinction explicit, though only after a challenge from Steve. It would on the other hand be a mistake to take these girls to be in any sense limited to such inexplicit uses of language, even though Bernstein and others have pointed to the over-use of pronouns in this way as a feature of the so-called 'Restricted Code'. Given other tasks these girls can be extremely explicit; part of our interest in this chapter is to find clues to when this is, and how it may be encouraged.

A closer look at this exchange, however, makes it seem less inadequate. Perhaps it is a mistake to read each girl's contribution as complete in itself. Let us make the attempt to read the first part of this passage as if it were one sentence, and not several sentences:

36. T	*The water comes up the straw*
37. C	*I wonder why*
39. B	*'cos of the air pressure*
42. C	*pressing down on the water*
43. T	*and it's* [= water] *coming up the tube*

Here I have omitted various repetitions and false starts, and with them one or two phrases which the speaker seemed to be addressing more to herself than contributing to the joint discussion. Even now the 'sentence' does not constitute a satisfactory explanation: in No. 39 it is not made explicit which air pressure is being referred to, and we are left to surmise that the 'it' in No. 43 refers to the water. Nevertheless, it can be seen from this way of considering their exchange that this group is at this moment genuinely collaborating in analysing the process. For example, it is Carol's 'I wonder why' which provokes Betty's explanation 'probably it's 'cos of the air pressure'; in one sense Carol's 'why' has been transmuted into Betty's 'because'. The subordination of one clause to another enables the speaker to represent to himself the relationship between two statements. For example, 'because of the air pressure' is related to Theresa's original statement 'The water comes up the straw' by the words 'because of', which signal a causal relationship. It is interesting to note that it is one girl's question which draws out the explanatory structure from the other. The task of elaborating meaning is here shared between members of the group; the questioning is part of the construction of thought through language. The point being made here is similar to that already made about Group II: the struggle to share their thinking forces a collaborative explicitness upon the group. Elaboration of language is not just a matter of each child's language habits, but can be fostered by a group's striving to think aloud together.

As we have seen, the two boys reached a higher level of explicitness than the girls in their discussion of the science tasks. Whereas the girls tended to 'explain' by using labels such as 'air pressure', and were slow to realize that it was necessary to specify where the pressure was operating, the boys of Group II qualified the expression every time one of them used it: 'the air pressure *outside*'; 'There's pressure created *inside the* bottle'; 'the pressure *on the other side of the apples*'. Let us now return to them for further illustration of the kinds of interaction that accompanied this explicitness. Steve's response to the fountain of water was a thoughtful 'Hey, that's good. Wonder how that's caused.' This ruminative inquiry, partly addressed to himself and partly to his more confident partner, is typical of his contribution throughout.

Meanwhile Glyn repeats the task, and sets off on an explanation:

34. G	Oh . . . Right. You see . . . er . . . you blow on this . . .
35. S	When you blow into the bottle . . .
36. G	Yes, there's pressure created inside the bottle and it forces . . . water up.
37. S	Why is it? Why squirt water out? Why does it come out of the straw though?
38. G	Because that's the only way it can come out.
39. S	Mm . . . OK.

Steve's tone sounds ironical when he substitutes for Glyn's inexplicit 'you blow on this' the more elaborated 'When you blow into the bottle ...' Conscious of the tape-recorder, he reminds Glyn that it is their task to formulate public statements. Glyn accepts the correction and continues, but Steve once again insists on a full explanation: 'Why does it come out of the straw?' His final 'Mm ... OK' sounds less than satisfied, so that it is no surprise that a few minutes later (after the task with the apples) he brings them back again to the fountain:

54. S		... I want to know though Glyn, when this ... you know when this experiment three ...
55. G		Yes.
56. S		You know when we blow down the straw ...
57. G		Yes.
56. S [cont.]		... and the water comes up ...
58. G		Yes.
56. S [cont.]		Well watch, and I'll do it again.
59. G		Not too much, then.
60. S		Yes, how come though, when it does come out ... I think some comes out by this straw here?
61. G		Oh well, that's 'cos it's not been tightly fixed ... most likely.
62. S		Yes. Well how come it doesn't make any bubbles at the bottom? Watch it, it doesn't.
63. G		Blow ... it does make bubbles ... look ... see bubbles ... coming up.
64. S		Mmm ... yes ... that's interesting.
65. G		Here, watch.
66. S		Yes ... Now what? ... Eee that's interesting.
67. G		That's because ... aah – oah [clearing throat] ... you've got no air pressure there to force the water out, so ... [inaudible].
68. S		So what happens if you put both fingers on it? If you put a finger on each end what would happen?

Steve's habit of questioning ('How come it doesn't make any bubbles?') has led him – after prompting from his friend – to perceive more truly. It was not that there were no bubbles on the previous occasions, but that his question, by turning his attention to the relevance of bubbles, has helped him this time to see them. Steve's learning here depends both on his question and on Glyn's reply, that is from their spoken interaction. Talking about the apparatus has made Steve see it differently. This has arisen from their interest in the subject matter and from their close relationship, but it has also been encouraged by their struggle to organize thoughts into sentences *that would mean something to persons not present.*

The latter part of the exchange quoted above well illustrates another characteristic of this pair. Not only do they formulate hypotheses and test them on the apparatus, but they even devise new ways of using the apparatus. It seems likely that when Glyn says 'Here, watch' (No. 65) he is loosening the stopper in the mouth of the flask, to show that this will prevent the fountain. Similarly they later devise ways of using the dangling apples to test ideas which go beyond the teacher's suggestions. No better illustration could be devised of an open approach to learning; but to notice this does not of course tell us how to foster such inventiveness in other groups. It would, however, be possible to design worksheets which explicitly encourage pupils to go beyond the tasks planned by the teacher, as Glyn and Steve did unprompted.

3. Discussion of a Poem

The poem *Warning* was chosen to provide a contrast with the work on air pressure. To comprehend this particular poem, a reader must achieve imaginative sympathy with a middle-aged woman's wish to engage in childish naughtiness, such as overeating and taking flowers from people's front gardens. At the same time he must realize that this childishness is the reverse side of a respectability which makes such behaviour impossible to her. Although this is easy enough for an adult, most children of this age find it difficult to hold at once within their sympathetic imagination two such contradictory groups of feelings. All children will have wished to be naughty; all will have learnt to check themselves from unacceptable behaviour. Their task was therefore to bring this existing experience to bear upon the poem. They were, however, given no more precise instruction than 'Talk about the poem in any way you want to.'

WARNING

When I am an old woman I shall wear purple
With a red hat which doesn't go, and doesn't suit me,
And I shall spend my pension on brandy and summer gloves
And satin sandals, and say we've no money for butter.
I shall sit on the pavement when I'm tired
And gobble up samples in shops and press alarm bells
And run my stick along the public railings
And make up for the sobriety of my youth.
I shall go out in my slippers in the rain
And pick the flowers in other people's gardens
And learn to spit.

You can wear terrible shirts and grow more fat
And eat three pounds of sausage at a go
Or only bread and pickle for a week
And hoard pens and pencils and beermats and things in boxes.

But meanwhile we must stay respectable
And must not shame the children; they mind more
Even than we do, being noticeable.
We will keep dry with sensible clothes and spend
According to good value, and do what's best
To bring the best for us and for our children.

But maybe I ought to practise a little now?
So people who know me are not too shocked and surprised
When suddenly I am old, and start to wear purple.

Jenny Joseph

Group IV boys apparently found the tape recorder too threatening to allow them to adopt a productive approach.

2. R	What do you think the poem's about, Tony?
3. A	Er . . . someone who's fairly young . . . er . . . Who's got children or grandchildren. [Whispers – pause]
4. J	Well what do you think it means by saying 'spend my pension on brandy and summer gloves . . . and satin sandals'?
5.	She'll waste her money. [Long pause]
6. J	What does she mean . . . And say 'we've no money for butter'?

7. R   Well she means . . . waste the money on some things and then just have no money for . . . other things . . . which are necessary.

One boy has appointed himself teacher and is asking the others to paraphrase lines from the poem. This is not an approach likely to increase their imaginative insight; these boys need help and practice in learning how to explore a poem and relate it to their own experience. Later there is one promising moment when one boy asks, 'Do you think she *would* eat three pounds of sausage at a go and only bread and pickle for a week after?' This could have been an invitation to a discussion of their own and other people's self-indulgence which would have brought them closer to one aspect of the poem. Another boy, however, interpreted it otherwise, and answered with a blunt 'No', making further discussion impossible. After a lengthy silence they went back to asking one another for paraphrases. The boys seemed unable or unwilling to explore possible meanings; they treated the poem as if each line of it had a 'right meaning'. This excluded the kind of discussion which might have helped them to make something of the poem, for their 'closed' approach can do nothing but leave them where they were when they started. This group was similarly 'closed' in their discussion of air pressure and Saxon settlements. This is not a simple matter of something called 'intelligence', however, as their IQ scores show. This group interpreted the recording session as something more threatening than the other groups did. One wonders whether they interpret lessons similarly.

In the work on air pressure, however, their failure to use dialogue as a mode of learning did not prevent Richard from saying some sensible things.

Well, when you suck you suck the air out and . . . then . . . there's only the milk . . . so the milk comes up the straw . . . the str . . . and . . . then . . . and . . . that . . . fetches . . . the milk down and . . . the air pressure is on the . . . milk as well.

Compared with the other groups they fail to utilize one another's suggestions as a basis for further thinking: Richard's remarks are just accepted with a 'You're right'.

Group I's approach to the poem is only a little more successful than Group IV's. They offer an accurate but chilly summary of the poem, which Theresa ends by saying 'It's all childish'. Surprisingly it is Group III who find a productive approach.

3. F		'When I am an old woman I shall wear purple with a red hat which doesn't go and doesn't suit me. I shall spend my pension on brandy and summer gloves.'
4. P		She sounds as if she's obstinate.
		[Sounds of amused agreement]
5. F		Sounds as if she's sick of being young as well.
6. L		Well she's got her ideas of being old hasn't she already? Don't think she'll *be* like that though.
7.		No.
6. L [cont.]		Well I wouldn't. [Laughs] Um 'Satin sandals and say we've no money for butter'. She hasn't got a lot of money I don't think.
8. F		She won't have with the pension.
9.		No.
10. L		'I'll gobble up samples in shops and press alarm bells.'
11.		I wonder what she wants to press alarm bells for.
12.		Perhaps she wants to be naughty as well as show off.
13.		Yes. [Both]

This group, like Group IV, keeps returning to the text of the poem – a very necessary part of constructing a meaning – but for purposes very different from Group IV's paraphrase. For example, Linda is willing to consider the voice in the poem as a potential person, 'Don't think she'd *be* like that though . . . Well I wouldn't.' This is a perfectly acceptable interpretation. An adult reader too would feel that the voice in the poem would never be likely to carry out her threats. But this is not directly to our purpose: what is important here is the mode of approach to the poem, viewing the character in a 'What if . . . ?' frame of mind. Group III are constructing from the poem a possible person and 'trying it out' against their own experience and against other parts of the poem. This hypothetical mode shows itself, for example, in Pauline's phrasing 'Sounds as if . . .' (No. 4), in the last three words of 'She hasn't got a lot of money *I don't think*', and in the 'I wonder' and 'Perhaps . . .' of Nos. 11 and 12. This is an 'open' approach in that it depends on the girls expecting to find the text meaningful and therefore being willing to stay with it long enough to construct a meaning for themselves. This would be equally true for a group working on quite different written texts, in history or science for example: unless they can be encouraged to stay and 'talk their way in' in an open fashion they are hardly likely to reach new understanding. A 'closed' approach has already been demonstrated to us in Group I's 'It's all childish'. Such a rejection makes it inevitable that they will leave the text without further progress in understanding it.

Group III's discussion continues:

14. P		'And pick flowers in other people's gardens.' Well she must have some sort of .. er belief that . . . got to get her own way back on other people.
15.		Yes. [Both]
		[Pause]
16. F		'I shall go out in my slippers in the rain.'
17. P		Well . . . I wonder what she means by that.
18. L		I will take the flowers . . . oh . . . 'And pick the flowers in other people's gardens . . . And learn to spit.'
19.		Ugh. [Both]
20. P		Well what does she want to spit at? There's nobody to spit at.
21. L		Well that's a dirty habit isn't it spitting . . . Well it is isn't it?
22.		Mm. Yes.

We see again their open approach: 'I wonder what she means by that?' and their readiness to bring their own values to bear on the matter of spitting. (Would this have happened if a teacher had been present?) What prevents them from making much progress is what we have already noted in their work on air pressure, that is, their tendency to accept uncritically whatever the other girls say. This contrasts with Group II who repeatedly take up what the other has said in order to modify or expand it.

The thirty-two substantial utterances which constitute Group III's discussion of the poem (including a part not quoted here; and excluding monosyllabic utterances) are distributed thus:

Statements – assertive   4
        – hypothetical   11

Questions	5
Repetition of text	12

Since all the questions, unlike those of Group IV, are essentially invitations to set up possibilities, we can group them with the hypothetical assertions and see that sixteen out of thirty-two utterances were in the hypothetical mode. This corroborates the intuitive judgement that the group's approach to the poem is very open, though this is not to say that with different kinds of material, or even a different poem, or with different instructions these same girls would not behave very differently. Indeed, they did so in the work on air.

Now, in pointing out the relative productiveness of the approach I have not, of course, used other criteria such as appropriateness and relevance. The fact that the group kept close to the text (twelve quotations) suggests that what they said was likely to be relevant. As for appropriateness, some of what they said would strike an adult reader as a useful comment on the poem, some not. It is necessary to add this in order to make it clear that I am *not* suggesting that openness is the only criterion which is relevant to deciding how fruitful a discussion is. In order to make progress in understanding apparatus or text without a teacher's guidance, a group must be capable of an open approach. So must a pupil when he works alone at a problem – and much secondary school work is done individually. I would argue that teachers should deliberately encourage and support their pupils in developing an open and hypothetical style of learning. Other styles may of course be more appropriate for other kinds of learning.

4. Saxon Settlements

I shall now consider how the same groups approached the historical task. The children were asked: 'What would a Saxon family first do when they approached English shores in order to settle?' They were also told that the discussion was a preparation for individual written work, in which they would write as if they themselves had been one of the invaders. Although this encouraged them to project themselves in imagination into the problems facing Saxon settlers in the sixth century, it did not encourage a dramatic approach. It rather invited them to ask questions on the model of 'What would they have done next?' than to assume the role of Saxons. One would expect this to encourage a hypothetical approach and this did, in fact, occur in all groups, even Group IV, though to a limited degree. Three of the four groups achieved their most productive discussions in this task. (Group II's discussion was not comparable; Steve was away from school and another boy took his place. I shall therefore not be able to use Group II in this part of the chapter.) I am not suggesting that the success of the Saxon Settlements discussions can entirely be put down to the topic's built-in pressure towards the hypothetical mode. The children were already well provided with relevant information, and had more to hand in the paragraph and sketch in front of them. Groups I, III and IV clearly found this task more within their capabilities than the others were, and approached it more positively, and indeed more intelligently.

Essentially the task was to construct in imagination the conditions under which a settlement would have been made. They therefore had to envisage a countryside very different from the England that they know, to recollect the kind of life that the Saxons were accustomed to, to recollect what tools they had at their disposal, and to predict what difficulties they would face. Children of this age do not find it easy to think realistically about a way of life other than their own: for example, one group had not realized that it might be necessary to clear land before ploughing it. An important part of their task, therefore, was to talk their way into such insight into the Saxons' situation that they would not fall into such failures of imagination. In some sense or other these children already possessed the necessary information, from former history lessons or from outside school – knowledge about ploughing, about waste land, about American pioneers, as well as about Saxons. What was now needed was to organize and relate it. By talking they could formulate and make conscious all this old knowledge, and make it available for use in the new task.

Let us first look at Group I doing this.

Dialogue	*Commentary*
28. B The Saxons used er timber didn't they to ...	Betty begins the sequence with what at first glance appears to be a statement. It functions however as
29. Yes	a hypothesis inviting further
28. B [cont.] ... to build houses?	exploration. (Implicitly: How should we take this into consideration in choosing a site for the village?)
30. T They cleared a ... Say they found a forest and you know they're probably all forests near the ... [inaudible]	Theresa takes up the implicit suggestion of the need for a site with a plentiful supply of timber. The 'Say' formula and the 'probably' invite the others to regard this contribution not as final but as open to qualification.
31. B Yes. They cleared it all away ... and then built all the little huts and brought all their animals and ...	Betty accepts the invitation and develops the idea further.
32. C ... All the family and that. They'd have to be pretty big huts.	Carol has not been following this line of thought, and now interrupts Betty with a dogmatic assertion which could lead in another direction.
33. T Yes.	This is politely acknowledged but taken no further.
34. B Why did they live in valleys?	Betty rescues the group from the dead end by raising a new question (provoked by the textbook illustration).
[Long pause]	
35. Aarh.	
36. T I suppose so ... so they ... they'd be sheltered.	The tentativeness with which Theresa eventually offers an answer is expressed both by her hesitations and by 'I suppose ...'
37. B Yes, for shelter ... and so er ... so there was less risk ... of being attacked I should think.	Betty accepts Theresa's answer but puts an alternative one of her own beside it; her hesitant delivery and the phrase 'I should think' disclaim any pretension to firm knowledge

			and implicitly invite further additions or qualifications.
38.	T	Yes.	Message received.
39.	C	Because they could only come from two directions.	Carol accepts the invitation and extends Betty's suggestion a step further.

This sequence shows a group which is working well together, asking useful questions and taking up one another's contributions in order to develop them. Expressions of tentativeness seem to play a part in encouraging this collaboration by keeping open the right of each of the girls to contribute. Betty asks questions (Nos. 28 and 34) which require constructive replies, and this was particularly important after Carol (No. 32) had broken the line of thought.

Questions of this kind are not only essential in keeping group discussion going, but are important to the child's own cognitive style. The pupil who is silently asking this kind of question when reading or listening to the teacher will gain more from lessons than the child who listens passively, yet most teachers do nothing to encourage such questioning. Such questions are almost entirely excluded from conventional lessons; it is the teacher who asks the questions and the pupils who may or may not 'know the answer'. In such a dialogue, exploratory and hypothetical questions or statements by pupils are very infrequent. I would argue that this kind of approach to learning should be encouraged, and that this cannot readily be done either in conventional teacher-class exchanges or by giving individual tasks to pupils.

Although I have taken this opportunity to argue that pupils' questioning should be deliberately encouraged, this passage was, in fact, quoted primarily to illustrate what is meant by 'learning by talking' and by 'an exploratory dialogue'. In the course of it, the three girls are re-articulating knowledge which in some sense they already possess. 'Re-articulating' here does not just mean 'putting into words'; the ideas which are mentioned – wooden houses, clearing timber, living in valleys – are being interrelated and given new meanings in relation to the question of where the Saxons would site a village. This kind of reinterpretation is an essential part of learning. The results of omitting this stage of learning can sometimes be seen in pupils' writing, when odds and ends of information are strung shapelessly together. I am not claiming only that such discussion makes for better writing, but that it represents a necessary process in learning. This kind of re-articulation of thought is more likely to happen in discussion than in the silence of individual thought, because in discussion all pupils have at least some awareness of the need to frame ideas so that others can understand them.

Group III's beginning is not auspicious:

1. P	Oh, well we got off . . . When we got off the boat I should think we should go to em . . . find a river.
2.	Yes.
1. P [cont.]	. . . where there's water . . . so that we can em . . .
3. F	Drink with.
1. P [cont.]	. . . Yes . . . and then look for see if there's any woods . . . near by the river . . . and then put our . . . all our belongings . . . bring them up there and . . . plant them down there.

Pauline has plenty to say, but has hardly begun to imagine the situation. The phrase 'got off the boat' suggests that she is thinking of a landing-stage, and 'go to find a river' shows how little she had taken in what her teacher had said about sailing up rivers. Her imaginary context for the settlement was short of furnishings, as is shown by the vagueness of 'all our belongings . . . bring them up there and . . . plant them down there.' But this should occasion no surprise: it must be true of most children of this age. No doubt one of the reasons which might be put forward for the study of history is for the better furnishing of children's imaginations, so that when they have to approach their own and other people's lives they may do so in the hypothetical mode, with a wide range of possibilities to put tentatively forward.

One of the other girls notices something of this lack of reality and suggests that they might travel up the river in a boat. This is noticeably different from their discussion of air pressure and of the poem: we noted in both cases their unwillingness to challenge one another. It seems possible that when this group of children feel unsure of themselves, uncertain whether they are in control of the task, they work for consensus, avoiding tensions and contradictions. Under those circumstances their exchanges tend to be brief, statements are accepted without elaboration, and ideas dealt with in a 'closed' simplifying way, without raising difficulties or attempting to put complex interrelations into words. This task, which they feel confident about, releases them in some degree from this uncertainty, with results that we shall now examine.

6. P   We could go up on the river on the boat . . .
6. [cont.] ⎱ . . . and then get off.
7. F   ⎰ Yes, but you see there might be er . . .
7. [cont.]   . . . wolves in the wood or . . . and they might . . . kill the sheep.
           [Long pause]
8.   Um . . . yes.
9. F   Well . . . we'd kill them. That . . . erm . . .
9. [cont.] ⎱ . . . yes that's what they did (at home).
10.   ⎰ Yes, but we wouldn't have any weapons, would we?
11. F   We'd have to make them.
12.   Make them.
13.   Yes.
14. F   We'd have brought all our belongings with us.

For the first time we hear Group III really collaborating to fashion an understanding of how the various aspects of the Saxons' position relate to one another. First Pauline suggests going up the river in a boat, then Frances points out the dangers of attack by wild animals upon their domestic stock. Her remark, though in a hypothetical form of words ('might'), is introduced by a blunt 'Yes but', and functions not so much as a contribution as a contradiction. Group II boys with their established trust of one another can cope with blunt contradictions, but most groups find them inhibiting. In the event, Group III here fell into a lengthy silence. In the end it is Frances herself who comes to the rescue with her story-book solution of killing the wolves; she then answers another girl's equally direct contradiction. They have dealt with the wolves but in the meantime have lost their positive impetus and fall into a silence punctuated by occasional embarrassed noises. Once again their social skills are inextricably involved in their use of language for learning: their ability to talk their way into understanding depends on their ability to cope with a dead-end of this kind, which is partly a social dead-end.

The problem is excellently solved by turning back to the page in the book: the decision to do so was made in whispers, which were partly inaudible. It should be kept in mind that before they began their discussion they had an opportunity to read the paragraph of text, and had spent a minute or two looking at the drawing of a Saxon village.

20. F	When it looks in this picture there's a boat there . . .	
21.	Mm.	
20. [cont.]	And the . . . they've got er erm . . . they've . . . built it next to the river.	
22. L	Yes. They've built a place next to the river.	
23.	Well.	
24. P	It looks like a canoe the boat doesn't it?	
25.	Yes.	
26. F	It's as if it's been a tree trunk and they've cut the middle out.	
27.	Mm.	
28. P	Well they've made little pen little pens for the um sheep so they can't . . .	
29.	Yes.	
28. P [cont.]	. . . so the wolves can't get them . . . or foxes or whatever.	

Unexpectedly they talk about the illustration as if they were seeing it for the first time. Aspects of the picture which had no meaning for them before, now leap out because their discussion has restructured their perception of the picture. Their previous disagreements about sailing up the river and about the safety of domestic animals enable them to find a new relevance in the positioning of the village beside a river, the presence of a boat, and in the pens for animals. Secondary school teachers sometimes talk of training their pupils to observe. This is not however a matter of training pupils to look. We observe not with our eyes alone but with our hypotheses.

This short exchange well illustrates two functions of verbalizing in learning: the preliminary discussion has reorganized the illustration for them, giving it new meaning; and they make this new meaning more consciously available to themselves and to one

another by putting it into words. I am here pointing to a reciprocal relationship between the visual representation and the verbal.
The visual representation provokes the children to verbalize what
they see *for one another*; here is the importance of the social
element in discussion. Verbal articulation in its turn reflects back
new meanings into the picture. We have seen before a similar
reciprocal relationship between verbalizing and physics apparatus, but only for Group II.

The last two paragraphs were concerned with the interaction
of verbal and visual representations upon cognitive learning. But
for Group III their successful return to the picture – their sense
that it had answered the problems they had encountered – has
important social effects.

30. F	Where would . . . ? I wonder where they'd get their food from?
31. P	Kill them.
32.	Ah yes.
33. P	Kill the animals.
34.	Yes.
35. L	And they'll have enough water.
36. F	And they'd be able to get the wood from the woods and erm make little fires.
37.	Yes.
38. L	And er . . . probably cook the er . . .
39.	Yes.
38. L [cont.]	food . . . and eat it all.

Frances turns away from the picture with a most productive
question, 'I wonder where they'd get their food from?' (She
possibly said this because no fields were shown in the sketch.)
Once again a hypothesis-demanding question of this kind proves
most fruitful. For the first time Group III is positively collaborating, picking up one another's questions and taking them further.

Before this question has been fairly settled, Frances raises
another which proves to be of a kind very unusual in children's
discussion.

40. F	Ooh what do you . . . what do you think was first thing that we'd do . . . when we'd got there and . . . found out what we'd do.

42. L	Find somewhere to build a house . . . just . . .
43. P	Do you think we'd start chopping trees down?
44.	Yes.
45.	Yes.
46. F	[At once] And we'd get all our equipment out. Yes . . . before night.
47.	Get our equipment . . .
48. F	And we could put up . . . erm . . . sort of . . . sort of little tent so that . . . for the night and then start working in the morning.
49. P	Yes.
50. L	Yes.
48. F [cont.]	. . . because it would have been a journey . . . before the night time.
51.	Mm.
52.	Well we'd . . . [inaudible]
53. P	Yes, but you see we won't have little tents if it was so . . . long ago would we?

Frances's question, 'What do you think was [the] first thing that we'd do when we'd got there?' is surprising because this was the very task which they had originally been given. To ask it is thus a request for recapitulation. Now anyone who has sat on an effective committee knows how valuable it is to stop everyone now and then to ask: 'Where have we got to?', in order to reach an explicit reformulation of ideas which have already been mentioned in a less explicit and organized way. It would seem to be extremely valuable for groups of children similarly to discuss work in two stages, one a less formulated and more exploratory one, and the second more planned and organized. In fact, the group does not accept the demand to recapitulate, and throws out a series of new suggestions with a fluency which one would hardly expect from Group III. The difficulty of deciding whether Saxons had tents brings the discussion to an end.

I have chosen to stay so long with Group III, quoting almost the whole of their discussion of the Saxon Settlement, because their dialogue so well shows what difficulties a group of average children face in working on their own, and also exemplifies a task which has brought the best out of them. My intention has been to show how children can, under certain circumstances, talk themselves into a better understanding, and at the same time to show that talking to learn needs preparation and support if it is to succeed. (Some notes about this are included as an appendix.)

We now turn to Group IV boys, who are a good deal less successful, though for a very different reason. Even on this third occasion Group IV still interpret the recording as a demand to put on a performance, rather than to use language to explore the possibilities of a topic. This emphasis upon language for performance rather than for exploration is, of course, communicated by many teachers when they treat classroom discussion as an opportunity for cross-questioning. (It is only fair to admit that I do not know how Group IV would have behaved if they had not known they were being recorded.) The other groups too were in a different sense 'presenting themselves' to the tape recorder: they would probably have behaved differently without it. But each of them at times succeeded in using language to make knowledge, whereas Group IV tended to use language to protect themselves.

If what is required is an authoritative statement, then a BBC news interviewer's style is appropriate, and this – after some preliminary whispering – Richard provides.

2. R   What would *you* do after *you'd* landed?

3. A   Well, first of all I'd . . . I'd find . . . er sort of a place to make a camp . . . village, and collect wood and cut trees down . . . collect straw . . . for hut roofs and that . . . make fences for cattle . . . er . . . What else would you do John?

4. J   Well . . . I'd make sure there were a fence going round . . . so no animals could get in . . . Then I'd start making the houses . . . and pens to keep the cattle in . . . Then start . . . ploughing the fields . . . to make crops . . . What would you do Richard?

5. R   First of all I'd find a suitable place to land and which would look nice to build your houses on it, next to the . . . river or the sea. And then explore the land around where you'd . . . you'd landed . . . before . . . you got settled down; and then . . . build a stockade . . . and . . . build your houses. And . . . get some fields ploughed . . . for crops . . . for the . . . winter.

We should perhaps view this ambiguously. For boys of average ability this is a not inadequate opening, relatively explicit and well-planned. Suggestions are given rational support: 'Get some fields ploughed ... for crops ... for the ... winter', the hesitations marking relatively complex thinking. But our phrase 'well-planned' warns us that language is not functioning for these boys as it was for Group III. They are not using language to explore the Saxons' situation, to shape what they know and relate it to the task – which is, as we have seen, a slow and complicated process. In a sense they are not talking to one another at all, and are certainly not collaborating in shaping new meanings. They are trying to proceed straight to a fully-organized 'final-draft' statement, and this means by-passing the necessary learning. Instead of using language for learning they are using it to communicate to the teacher that they are obedient pupils, that they 'know the answer'. I have already suggested that these boys may perceive the recording as more threatening than the other groups did, and therefore retreat into a closed approach. Such a perception would not be unreasonable: a considerable part of children's time in school is spent in feeding back to teachers what the teachers have already given out. It is unusual for them to be expected to adopt a hypothetical stance, to throw out ideas tentatively, or to collaborate in building on other people's formulations. These boys may well wonder what the catch is. Unfortunately their defensiveness may hinder parts of their learning, since for some purposes the hypothetical mode is essential. The girls of Group I (as we shall see) move easily and quickly from the strategies needed for thinking aloud to those needed to satisfy the teacher; it is at least conceivable that this is one of the reasons why their science teacher saw them as 'good at science'.

On first impression, Group I's approach to the task is encouraging: if this had happened in a lesson one would have thought that it was going well.

> 4. C   When the boat lands the first thing they'd have to do ...
> be ... to find ... em place where they can build a house,
> and probably later on have ... fields of their ... crops
> and ... places ...

4. C [cont.] ⎰ ... to keep ... em ...
5. B ⎱ ⎰ They'd probably look round first.
4. C [cont.] ... cattle and [inaudible] ... pigs and things.
6. T But they'd have to be out of the way of swamps and things ... so they wouldn't be in any danger.
7. B You could say that when they arrived there they wouldn't use the ... em ... Roman things ... that had already been put there.
8. T They wouldn't go near them because they were scared of the old Roman villages.[1]
9. C And ... th' ... they would p – probably ... keep away from the ... Roman towns erm ... the ... temples and that w – were mysterious and frightening places to them ...
10. C And ... they were em ...
11. T Yes.
10. C [cont.] ... they didn't understand things like that.
12. B Yes ... probably they were ... an ...
13. C And they've got to take ...
12. B [cont.] ... under-educated. [Amused]
13. C [cont.] ... and they've got to take care of all their animals and things because ... if they ... went too far from home they could die of exposure.
14. B All that was in their old land, wasn't it?
15. C No.
16. Hmm ... [Long pause]

Yet on what is this approval based? The passage does not read like a conventional 'history essay'. Why should it? These girls are still in the process of organizing their thoughts. The level of interaction is high: although remarks follow one another in quick succession, each one is related to something that has gone before. We should not be disturbed by an imprecise phrase such as 'Roman things'; an acceptable phrase such as 'the remains of Romano-British civilization' would be no more explicit. Moreover, the other two girls quickly go on to specify 'villages' and 'towns and temples', which is quite explicit enough for their present purpose. If this conversation is closely organized, it should be possible to demonstrate *how* it is organized. This would

1. The transcription is uncertain here: the word may be 'religions' not 'villages'.

amount to showing how this group of girls is using language to organize their thinking about this topic. The following diagram is an attempt to show the structure of thought in the discussion.

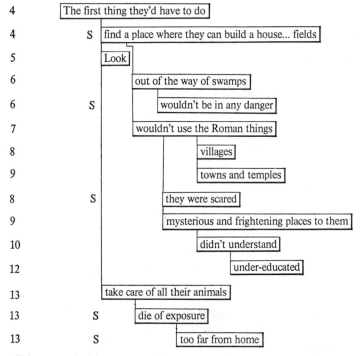

Whenever the idea expressed in one contribution has been elaborated by a later contribution, I have linked the two with a vertical line, shifting the second contribution one space to the right to show that it is in some sense subordinated to the first.

This is a crude way of representing very complex relationships. It differs from the 'clause analysis' which readers will remember from their schooldays in that it is concerned not with the structure within a sentence, but with the relationship between the meanings of sentences spoken by different people. Thus, although some of the ideas are linked together by conjunctions such as 'because' and 'if' – that is, they are 'subordinated' in the grammarian's sense of the word – most of the others are not formally linked. It may help the reader to consider the diagram item by item. Several of the items in the diagram are very much compressed versions of what was actually said, so the reader is invited to refer back from the diagram to the passage from time to time.

The whole section gains its unity from the teacher's question about what the Saxons would do first, and this appears in Carol's opening remark as: 'When the boat lands *the first thing they'd have to do* . . .' Three answers are offered to the teacher's question and these three are shown as subordinated to Carol's phrase. First Carol herself suggests that the Saxons would '*find a place where they can build a house*'. (In fact, she continues to elaborate this by adding that they would have fields for crops and animals, but I have omitted this to simplify the diagram.) Then Betty suggests that the Saxons would '*look around*' first, but the others ignore this. Theresa takes up Carol's idea of finding a place for a house and suggests one criterion for placing it: '*out of the way of swamps*', and elaborates this by giving the reason that they '*wouldn't be in any danger*'. Betty now offers a second criterion for placing the house, and this is shown as parallel with the first criterion. She says, 'They *wouldn't use the Roman things.*' The vagueness of the word 'things' may trouble the others, since during the next two utterances they specify Roman '*villages*' and '*towns and temples*'. Indeed, the section from No. 7 to No. 12 is very closely knit as the girls quickly elaborate what seems to be a familiar idea. Carol explains that to the Saxons the remains of Roman settlements were '*mysterious and frightening places*' because 'they didn't understand things like that', to which Betty jokingly adds that they were 'under-educated'. After this quite lengthy expansion of Betty's original mention of 'Roman things' they return to the original question; Carol reminds them that as well as finding a place for a house the Saxons would have to '*take care of all their animals*' and this she herself elaborates.

This analysis has been undertaken to show how complex the collaborative planning can be when a group is working well together; it does not follow that because dialogue is improvised it is therefore shapeless. Group I is here organizing with considerable success a complex body of information. I am not, of course, saying that they therefore 'possess' this structure in some kind of permanent form. The purpose of this analysis was to give some kind of permanence to the fragile structures of understanding set up momentarily in dialogue. We can only recapture them by stopping and looking back.

It is of interest that syntactical subordination is not the only form of elaboration possible. When Betty says (No. 12) 'Yes . . . probably they were . . . under-educated,' we have no difficulty in understanding that she means 'The Roman villages were mysterious and frightening places to the Saxons *because* they were under-educated'. Her omission of the syntactical subordinator 'because' makes no difference whatsoever to the function of the sentence. Indeed, most of the structure we have been analysing is held together in this non-syntactical way. Out of the fourteen 'subordinations' shown in the diagram, only five are marked syntactically. (In the diagram the syntactically marked subordinations are preceded by 'S'.) This is of some theoretical interest because of the current emphasis by Bernstein and others on the importance of elaboration by syntactical means for the organizing of thought. Of particular interest is the way the other girls expand Betty's phrase 'Roman things'. It may be that in the kind of discussion that we are calling 'exploratory' this looser and less explicit way of linking ideas encourages flexibility and the 'trying out' of half-formed thoughts. It would be unfortunate if emphasis upon syntactical elaboration made us undervalue exploratory dialogue.

One unfortunate effect of Bernstein's work has been to make some teachers believe that there are some pupils who 'use a restricted code' and that nothing can be done about it. The dialogues which we have been examining have shown that 'elaboration' is not just an ability possessed by an individual, since we have seen groups collaborating in using language to elaborate and relate. Bernstein himself has written: 'I must emphasize that because the code is restricted it does not mean that speakers at no time will use elaborated speech variants.'[2] If it could be shown that groups can *learn* to elaborate, this would be an important

2. 'Social Class Language and Socialization', reprinted in B. Bernstein (ed.) (1971), *Class, Codes and Control*, Vol. 1, Routledge & Kegan Paul.

educational finding. I cannot attempt so far-reaching a task on the present limited evidence, however. These recordings indicate no more than that the same group of pupils uses language to elaborate thought far more successfully on some occasions than others.

5. Strategies of Learning

I began by asking, 'What strategies do groups of pupils adopt when set interpretative tasks, and which of these are more profitable?' It is now possible to offer tentative replies, in the way of a summary of the preceding three sections.

a) *Open Approach to Tasks*

The more successful approach, which I have called 'open', is characterized most clearly by the use of the hypothetical mode: the pupils ask questions of one another of a kind which invite surmise and discussion. They ask ruminative questions of themselves, and their statements are tentative, exploratory, inviting elaboration by others. They freely find new questions to ask of one another, and see further possibilities in the materials beyond what the task explicitly requires. They persevere in trying to organize their ideas, so that discussions are often lengthy. They sometimes turn back in order to summarize or repeat what has already been said.

This open approach implies a collaborative social relationship in which pupils make frequent use of one another's contributions by extending or modifying them. They address one another directly, sometimes by name, and occasionally ask one another to explain or extend what they have already said. They deal with disagreement in open discussion in order to reach verbal clarification of the difference.

b) *Closed Approach to Tasks*

A group using the approach which I have called 'closed' tends to limit their activities to whatever has been explicitly asked for. They seldom ask questions of their own, and when they do these questions ask for limited pieces of information rather than for exploratory discussion. Their replies to the tasks set tend to be confined to labelling processes rather than analysing them. Their contributions tend to be assertions, which often seem dogmatic, and these lead to acceptance or rejection rather than to extension or modification by others.

Two alternative patterns of social relationships occurred with the closed approach:

i) *Consensus*. In this pattern the pupils seldom express disagreement with one another's opinions. When disagreement does occur it often leads to a breakdown in the work. Pupils seldom refer directly to previous contributions to discussion and are satisfied with a low level of explanation. Each topic of discussion lasts only a short time; pupils seem more interested in preserving smooth relationships than in carrying out the task.

ii) *Ritual*. In this pattern the questions and answers are ritualized, so that there is no real exchange of information or opinions. Pupils seldom take up anything previously said. The activity amounts to 'putting on a show' for an outsider, so that there is little or no engagement with the topic.

c) *Orientation to Audience*

Cutting across the open and closed approaches to learning, and not directly related to them, came the pupils' varying awareness of the larger audience implied by the tape-recorder. Ignoring this led to an *exploratory* 'talking to oneself' – or to one's close friends; high awareness led to the deliberately *public presentation* of ideas.

d) *What Determines the Approach?*

In a study of this kind nothing more than surmises is possible.

i) The approach made by Groups I, II and III varied with the three tasks; only Group IV retained a 'closed' and 'ritualized' approach throughout. Thus, choice of approach cannot be put down solely to the pupils' differences in intelligence or articulateness.

ii) The Saxon Settlement called out more open approaches than either of the other tasks. This might be because the task was easier, or because the pupils had more relevant information, or because they understood more clearly what was required of them, or because in its nature the task encouraged a hypothetical approach.

iii) The more uncertain Groups I and III were about their competence in the task the more they tended to use a closed approach and to aim at consensus.

iv) Whereas Group II gained a greater explicitness from their awareness of audience, Group IV's attempt at public presentation led them to a closed approach and ritualized relationships. It seems possible that awareness of audience inhibits an open approach for some pupils.

e) *The Hypothetical Mode*

A number of students of children's language have singled out tentativeness as an important quality. For example, Walter Loban, who studied the language of a group of children in California as it developed during their school years, wrote:

Those subjects who proved to have the greatest power over language ... were the subjects who most frequently used language to express tentativeness ... supposition, hypotheses and conditional statements.[3]

The matter is not a simple one. How are we to recognize 'power over language'? It is not impossible that in isolating tentativeness we are merely pointing to a characteristic of the speech habits of middle-class people. Turner and Pickvance[4] have shown that in a sample of five-year-old children those from middle-class homes used forms of words expressing uncertainty far more frequently than those from working-class homes. But how important are words like 'might' or 'perhaps'? Do they always express a hypo-

3. Loban, W. D. (1963), *The Language of Elementary School Children*, Research Report No. 1, National Council of Teachers of English, Champaign, Illinois.
4. Turner, G. J. and Pickvance, R. E. (1971), 'Social Class Differences in the Expression of Uncertainty in Five Year Old Children', in B. Bernstein (ed.), *Class, Codes and Control*, Vol. 2, Routledge & Kegan Paul, (1973.)

thetical strategy, or are they sometimes mere verbal habits that do not affect the speaker's thinking? We often signal uncertainty through the intonation patterns of our speech, and these may be more important than the forms of words which Turner and Pickvance counted, and which I have been discussing.

It has been the American sociologist William Labov who has put these doubts most forcefully into words. He describes some of the forms which I have associated with the hypothetical mode as 'the bench marks of hemming and hawing, backing and filling'. And he issues the warning: 'Before we impose middle-class verbal style upon children from other cultural groups, we should find out how much of this is useful for the main work of analysing and generalizing, and how much is merely stylistic – or even dysfunctional.'[5]

These doubts should persuade us to a certain tentativeness of our own in using the ideas expressed in this chapter. It seems likely, however, that any group of people faced with a problem which is to be solved collaboratively will do well to approach it in the hypothetical mode. And even when an individual is attempting to solve a problem, he will not be able to use any feedback available – he will not be able to learn from his mistakes – if he clings dogmatically to first impressions. What is not so clear is whether tentative forms of words are always vehicles for hypothetical cognitive strategies: and this must at present remain a hypothesis.

6. The Teacher Joins In

So far I have presented learning as something which the pupil does, and which the teacher cannot do for him. I have argued that in finding words to express ideas and feelings to others he will be reshaping them for himself. It cannot be assumed, however, that this reshaping will go on whenever a group of pupils

5. Labov, W. (1970), 'The Logic of Nonstandard English'. Reprinted in A. Cashdan and E. Grugeon (eds.) (1972), *Language in Education*, Routledge & Kegan Paul.

is put together; planning is necessary. Some tasks may raise the level of performance of all groups; another task may raise one group above its usual level; another may be so vague, or so difficult, that it leaves all groups floundering. The quality of the discussion – and therefore the quality of the learning – is not determined solely by the ability of the pupils. The nature of the task, their familiarity with the subject matter, their confidence in themselves, their sense of what is expected of them, all these affect the quality of the discussion, and these are all open to influence by the teacher. In this section we are concerned with what the teacher can do to contribute to successful discussion by taking part in it.

With each of the three tasks, as soon as a group indicated that their discussion had ended, the teacher who had set the task joined in, asked for their conclusions, and then briefly attempted to take the discussion further. I shall assume that the teacher matches what the children say with whatever he wished them to learn, and then tries to lead them towards the latter. By considering what happens – especially in comparison with the same group without a teacher – we can hope to learn something of the effect of the teacher's participation.

The instructions relating to the air pressure apparatus contained the sentence: 'Remember to give an explanation *using the correct words*.' One can understand, of course, that a teacher of science might be concerned to encourage his pupils to use the terminology of his subject. He will, however, be more interested in whether they can use the scientific concepts for thinking with than in whether they can say words. The difficulty about telling children to use 'the correct words' is that they may interpret it as an instruction about words rather than about concepts. If so, it may seem to them equivalent to telling them to make noises which sound scientific. We have seen how some of the children used 'vacuum' and 'air pressure' as vague labels which absolved them from thinking more analytically about the processes referred to. It is conceivable that the instructions encouraged this. If we emphasize the use of stylistically appropriate language before pupils have sorted out how to use concepts, we may actually inhibit development. The attempt to predetermine the terms which the children use may prevent them from using language to learn with: the control affects the learning.

When he faced each of the groups, the science teacher showed clearly what uses of language he wanted, and was quick to challenge any vague phrase-spinning, whether in technical language or in everyday words. In Group I he asks Theresa why he is able to drink milk through a straw, and she replies, 'Because you're sucking in through the hole in the bottom and it's ... well ... er ...', he immediately asks, 'What exactly forces the milk up the tube?' He then refused to accept the unanalysed concept 'sucking' and required Theresa to break down the process. The formulation of his question ('forces the milk up the tube') requires his pupils to revise the conceptual framework with which they are considering the milk-drinking, and to redefine 'sucking' in terms of forces operating in particular directions upon particular materials. To do this they will have to be much more explicit, so the question is implicitly a demand for a greater elaboration in language.

We have already noticed that Group I, unlike Group II, when they speak of 'air pressure' usually fail to specify where this pressure is. The teacher pounces on this.

Teacher	... Come on, describe this one to me ... I can't do it because there's no water left in here, is there; you've used it all up ... [girls' laughter] ... but you can describe it to me, can't you?
24. B	Em ... well ... Theresa blew down it and it bubbled, and then she took em ... her mouth away, and it all came up because of the air pressure.
Teacher	Which air pressure?
25. B	The ... er ... inside the bottle.
26.	... Inside the bottle.
Teacher	Alright! Now why didn't it come up before then? ... Before we blew the air in why didn't it come up?
27. C 28. T	Sir, 'cos ... em ... 'cos there wasn't enough air ... air pressure.
	[Clash of voices—words not transcribed].
28. T [cont.]	There wasn't enough air in, but when you blew into it ... there was more air in and it came up.

Teacher	And it forced it . . . Why did it stop? . . . At what point did it stop? . . . It's not going now . . . why isn't it going now?
29. T	'Cos there's no air left in.
Teacher	Well there's still the air left in; but what can you tell me about the air out here and the air in here?
30. C	Sir, the air outside is stronger than the air in the bottle.

His sequence of questions – 'Which air pressure?' 'Why didn't it come up before?' 'Why did it stop?' 'At what point did it stop?' – is designed to persuade the girls to analyse the process systematically. He is providing the questions which they failed to ask of themselves.

Similarly with Group III his questions were directed towards persuading the girls to reconsider what they had said, to 'recode' it, in Bruner's formulation.

Teacher	Now who's going to have a bash at explaining to me what actually happens . . . when we drink milk?
4. F	Er . . . well you suck all the air . . . out . . . er . . . out of this milk, and er the milk the suction from the air the milk comes up to the top.
Teacher	The suction from the air. Now what do we mean by the suction from the air?

For Frances the phrase 'the suction from the air' was functioning to label off an area of experience, whereas the teacher, in questioning the girls, is asking them to use language differently, as an instrument to break down and restructure that area.

Both with this group and Group IV he went far towards doing the restructuring for them. In discussing with Group III the fountain from the stoppered jar he asked:

Teacher	Well, we blew into it, and what happened?
27. F ⎱	All the water came out of the straw.
28. P ⎰	The water came out of the s – top.
Teacher	All came out! Now why? Come on! This one's easy.
29. F	'Cos when you were blowing bubbles in, all the . . . air came up the straw . . . and water with it.
Teacher	Ooh no! I don't think that's quite right. When we blew air through here . . . where did the air go?

30.	
31.	[Together] Into the bottle.
32.	

Teacher   Into the bottle! So was there more air in here or less air?

33.	
34.	[Together] More.

Teacher   More air, wasn't there? There was a lot more air in here. Now this air . . . wanted to do what?

35.		Get out
36.	[Clash of voices]	Push water . . .

36. [cont.]   . . . push water outside to get room for itself.

Teacher   Yes, ah. That's a very good answer.

The teacher broke down the problem most skilfully into three stages. First, he wanted them to consider all the relevant information, and therefore asked the girls what happened to the air blown in. Second, he asked them to be explicit about the higher pressure inside the jar. Third, he asked them to consider the effect of the higher pressure. Thus, 'air pressure', instead of being a general label for the whole process, became a central term relating the input of the first stage to the output of the third. It is difficult to estimate the effect of this kind of teaching in which the teacher provides a framework for the children to fill in. Certainly they now have a better understanding of this phenomenon; moreover, they have been given an excellent model for the analysis of a physical process by a rational use of language. What is not so certain is whether it has helped them to be more actively analytical when next they are faced with a task in physics, alone or in a group.

It would be wrong to think that this urging of pupils towards the explicit analysis of general statements only happens in science, where the teacher is communicating well-defined and public patterns of thought. Although in history the teacher was not dealing in precisely defined concepts, his task, too, required the pupils to analyse ideas referred to by general labels. Consider 'start work' in the following discussion with Group III:

4. P   We'd get out and put all our belongings on the . . . thing . . . and . . . see that everything's out . . . and look

for trees and ... make up a little tent for the night and then start work the next day.

Teacher	Yes. What sort of work could you do then?
5. L ⎫ 6. F ⎭	Make a harbour Cut down trees and things like that.
Teacher	Hm. Why?
7. P	To make the houses and ...
Teacher	Yes?
7. P [cont.]	Make a fence for the animals.
Teacher	Hm.
8. L ⎫ 9. F ⎭	And kill animals ... er ... for food. ... for food.
Teacher	Yes?
10. P	And collect wood to make a fire ... to cook the food on.

Group III began at their vaguest with 'put all our belongings on the thing', 'see that everything's out', and 'start work'. These vague labels assume an agreement about what the Saxons possessed, the terrain they were arriving in, and what needed to be done. Yet these things are precisely what the task required the pupils to construct; Group III's assumption of consensus is getting between them and the task in hand. So the teacher challenges them with 'What sort of work would you do?' and this proves a most productive question, calling out explicit and well-organized suggestions. He wisely limits his own part in this to making encouraging noises.

It might be supposed from this that groups were always more explicit when talking to teachers, and that for this reason class discussion would be generally more valuable than small-group discussion, in spite of the small proportion of a class which can take active part in the former. With our four groups it did not seem to be the case that the teacher's questioning always brought out greater explicitness. Indeed three of the groups show a low level of explicitness on at least one occasion, in spite of the teacher's efforts.

11. B	Well, they'd need to shelter from ... em ... some things.
12. T	Animals and weather.
Teacher	Animals and what? ... What else might they want to shelter from?
13.	Weather.

14.	Weather.
Teacher	Weather, hm-mm, yes. True! OK, so the first step, as you say, is spending the night as comfortably as possible. Then what? ... Following day. Imagine it's a nice sunny day like this. What's the first sort of thing that you're going to do?
15.	Have a meal.
Teacher	Right.
16.	Yes.
Teacher	Hm-mm.
17. B	And then collect er food ... Chop down trees for ... houses.

It is hard to believe that this is the same Group I who talked with such fluency and explicitness on this same subject. How can we account for the single-word answers, the failure to 'think aloud', the clipped sentences without grammatical subjects ('Chop down trees for houses')? It is not that the history teacher has been leaning heavily on them; he asks helpful questions and his style is encouraging and unhurried. Nor is this a momentary lapse of attention: Group I continues in this way for most of the conversation. It is almost as if the girls of Group I have stopped using language for thinking with. They have done their own sorting out, and they feel no urgency to explain to their teacher what he knows already. Showing him that they have done their work is very different from explaining things to themselves and to one another.

We have just seen how well Group III responded to their teacher's question about the kind of work the Saxons would do. A few minutes later a similar question produced a quite different result.

Teacher	What would they be looking for, Pauline?
21. P ⎫ 22. F ⎭	Flat land.
Teacher	And what else? Anything else?
23.	Em.
Teacher	The land with ...
24. F	[Interjecting] Good soil.
Teacher	Good. Yes ... what else?
25.	Em. [Long pause]

26. L	They're looking for [softly] . . .
27. F	[Interjecting] Trees.
26. [cont.]	. . . Ah. Trees.
Teacher	What do you want? Trees or not?
28. P	They'd cut those down and use it 'cause trees fertilize the soil . . . doesn't it?

This is an even more extreme failure to be explicit, yet it is not untypical of many exchanges which occur when a teacher asks questions of his whole class, and could easily be paralleled from recordings of lessons made elsewhere. These girls are using language in this way *because they interpret the demands of the situation differently* from the way they interpreted it when alone. Since the 'task' is still the same, this is the only possible explanation. How then are they interpreting the situation? The answer to this can only be a surmise. What seems to have happened here is that the girls have assumed that when the teacher asks 'What would they be looking for?' he is not asking them to explore possible replies, or to set up hypotheses for the others to play with, but is asking them to guess certain answers ready-made in his mind. If this surmise is true, it would explain their failure to use language in an 'open' and *exploratory* way; very brief replies ('Flat land') would suffice to show the teacher that they could give the 'right' answers. Quite unintentionally, the teacher has shifted Group III away from the hypothetical mode to a mode of closed assertions which can be scored right or wrong. This perhaps goes some way to help explain Group I's relative inexplicitness in the previously quoted passage too.

When pupils work alone their discussion may be inconclusive or inexplicit or superficial: we have seen all of these faults above. Every teacher wishes to rush in and ask the well-placed question, and – as we have seen – this is sometimes helpful. But just as often it has the reverse effect. Taking the initiative out of the pupils' hands may reduce their learning from an active organizing of knowledge to a mere mimicry of the teacher – catching his style of phrase or guessing what he has in mind. Mimicry is a part of learning, but it is very different from the kind of exploratory learning which I have illustrated.

Moreover, there are other limitations to teacher-dominated

learning. Questions can go very wrong, because of a teacher's failure to project himself into his pupils' viewpoint. Competition for the teacher's attention can hinder learning. The lively and able Glyn of Group II dominated the discussion with each teacher, while Steve – so valuable to Glyn when they worked as a pair – hardly got a word in. When we consider children working in small groups we tend to compare their discussion with an idealized teacher-pupil dialogue, forgetting how often this falls below the ideal even for an experienced teacher, and forgetting too that it compels most of the class to listen in silence. Moreover, as we have shown, the very presence of a teacher alters the way in which pupils use language, so that they are more likely to be aiming at 'answers' which will gain approval than using language to reshape knowledge. Only the most skilful teaching can avoid this.

It therefore seems likely that the language strategies which this chapter has illustrated cannot be encouraged by teaching methods which rely entirely upon teacher-class dialogue. Teachers should avoid on the one hand a teacher domination that discourages pupils from active learning, and on the other the abandonment of pupils to their own devices. Thrown in at the deep end, some pupils might learn something, but teachers would be abdicating their duty if they did not take some responsibility for what their pupils learn.

Chapter Three
Ways of Thinking about Classroom Learning

1. School Knowledge and Action Knowledge

When the teacher's authority was temporarily withdrawn by organizing children in small groups, a new communication system took over, one which the children progressively shaped in the course of their discussions. By removing one set of expectations I required them to negotiate others. Since the new strategies were not controlled by a teacher they were more likely to be responsive to the learners' sense of what was needed – responsive to what they already knew, to their interpretation of the tasks they had been given, and to their intuitions about what constituted useful ways of tackling those tasks. It is this *responsiveness to the learner's view of what is required* that makes the study of small-group discussions so informative.

In writing about the group discussions I have so far been content to assume an understanding of the nature of the learning which the children were engaged in. One difficulty in thinking about knowledge is that it is both 'out there' in the world and 'in here' in ourselves. The fact that it is 'out there' and known to a teacher doesn't mean that he can give it to children merely by telling them. Getting the knowledge from 'out there' to 'in here' is something for the child himself to do: the art of teaching is knowing how to help him to do it. What we have been doing is listening to children using one of the means at their disposal in making knowledge their own, that is, reshaping it in talking.

Let us consider this in another way. Imagine two children who have been learning about animals' diet and teeth. One child, if asked the right question, can tell you that some animals eat meat, some vegetable foods, and some both, and that this matches differences in their teeth. The other child has learnt that wild cats eat meat, knows that his own cat at home has a mixed diet, and wonders what effect this will have on his teeth. The first child in one sense 'knows' about diet and teeth but can only use it in the classroom; it is still 'school knowledge'. The other child is beginning to incorporate the information into the inner map of reality on which his actions are based, his 'action knowledge'. Most teachers will agree that though a great deal of learning in school begins as school knowledge, it is not much use for anything (except perhaps examinations) until it becomes part of the learner's action knowledge. We educate children in order to change their behaviour by changing their view of the world. We want to change the way they perceive the world they live in, not so that they will carry out our purposes, but so that they can formulate their own purposes, and estimate their value.

I am not, of course, wishing to imply that teachers have no part to play. Indeed, I have already said in discussing the four groups that the school contributed a great deal to the usefulness of their discussions. It was teachers who selected the historical topic, who set up the air pressure apparatus and who framed tasks for the pupils to address themselves to. More importantly, it was teachers (as well as other adults) who had over previous years listened attentively to what children said, and encouraged them to use language to explore ideas.

To give adults no part in children's education is to expect the children to construct the whole of human knowledge for themselves. The central problem of teaching is how to put adult knowledge at children's disposal so that it does not become a strait-jacket. How can children learn to use for their own ends the knowledge which adults present to them? Piaget puts it in this way:

In some cases, what is transmitted by instruction is well assimilated by the child because it represents an extension of some spontaneous constructions of his own. In such cases his development is accelerated. But in other cases the gifts of instruction are presented too soon or too late, or in a manner that precludes assimilation because it does not fit in with the child's spontaneous constructions. Then the child's development is impeded, or even deflected into barrenness, as so often happens in the teaching of the exact sciences. Therefore I do not believe . . . that new concepts, even at school level, are always acquired through adult didactic intervention. This may occur, but there is a much more productive form of instruction: the so-called 'active' schools endeavour to create situations that, while not 'spontaneous' in themselves, evoke spontaneous elaboration on the part of the child, if one manages both to spark his interest and to present the problem in such a way that it corresponds to the structures he had already formed himself.[1]

This directs our attention to the relationship between what the learner knows already and the new system being presented to him. To learn is to develop relationships between them, and this can only be done by the learner himself. This is why pupils' talk is important, in that it is a major means by which learners explore the relationship between what they already know, and new observations or interpretations which they meet.

Piaget used the expression 'spontaneous constructions' to refer to the learner's existing knowledge, and contrasts this with the 'non-spontaneous' constructions presented by teachers. This formulation is potentially misleading, however. The knowledge with which a child approaches school tasks will inevitably contain substantial elements which he has taken over from adults. On the other hand, all knowledge has to be actively incorporated into the way he interprets the world, or it will be of little value. This is why I have preferred to make the distinction between 'school' and 'action' knowledge.

School knowledge is the knowledge which someone else presents to us. We partly grasp it, enough to answer the teacher's questions, to do exercises, or to answer examination questions, but it remains someone else's knowledge, not ours. If we never use this knowledge we probably forget it. In so far as we use knowledge for our own purposes however we begin to incorporate it into our view of the world, and to use parts of it to cope with the exigencies of living. Once the knowledge becomes incorporated into that view of the world on which our actions are based I would say that it has become 'action knowledge'.

1. Piaget, J. (1962), 'Comments on Vygotsky's Critical Remarks Concerning *The Language and Thought of the Child* and *Judgment and Reasoning in the Child*', an appendix to Vygotsky, L. S. (1962), *Thought and Language*, Massachusetts Institute of Technology Press.

What I am calling 'action knowledge' is not necessarily what primary school teachers refer to when they speak of 'learning by doing'. The emphasis in early childhood education upon learning from first-hand sensory experience, and especially from the handling of materials, arises from developmental theories such as Piaget's which posit that cognition begins when a child symbolizes reality to himself in terms of what he can do to it. Thus teachers of young children seek to give their pupils the experience of manipulating things before expecting them to deal with them in words: a concept first intuited by handling things is later sharpened and brought to awareness by being talked about. This is not what I intend by the phrase 'action knowledge' which here refers to pupils' *assimilation of knowledge to their own purposes*. A child can handle things without in the least finding them relevant to his purposes; this would be manipulation but not action. A child can try to talk someone into doing what he wants: this would be action but not manipulation. When an infant pours water, or an adolescent carries out a chromatographic analysis, these may imply action – but they may not. Of the two, it is action that I am concerned with here.

An important task for the learner in school is that of converting school knowledge into action knowledge. Talk and writing are of great importance here, because they provide means of testing out school knowledge against the action knowledge. For example, in the discussion of the Saxon Settlement the children were trying to relate what they had learnt in history lessons with existing knowledge of diverse kinds. In his novel *Hard Times* Dickens illustrates the difference between school and action knowledge by means of the character, Cissy Jupe. Cissy had spent her life amongst circus horses, but found no meaning in the accredited definition of a horse as 'quadruped, graminivorous . . .' etc., since this bore upon biologists' purposes in categorizing animals and not upon any purposes which she could conceive of. The gap between the two was too wide to be crossed.

To understand the problems faced by learners we have to know not only the tasks presented to them from the teacher's point of view but also what in their existing view of things will have to be changed in order to cope with the new knowledge, or solve a new problem. In one sense only the learner himself has this information, and he does not know he knows it. This is why it is important for the learner to talk or write or otherwise represent the problem to himself, and why his active participation is crucial. What are the contexts in which the learner is most encouraged to take responsibility for learning?

How can we help children perceive the world differently? How does school-learnt knowledge become incorporated in the child's expectations about the real world? Children vary a great deal in the amount of help they need; our groups differed greatly in the extent to which they set up hypotheses, and tested them, or returned again to talk their way into understanding. Of course, language is not the only means of learning but as children become older it becomes more important, especially in the self-aware kinds of learning that are expected of them in secondary schools.

What we can expect, as children use language to make knowledge their own, is a two-way process: they will be both putting old familiar experience into words in order to see new patterns in it *and* trying to make sense of new experience by finding a way of relating it to the old. We saw the first of these when Group I girls were applying their historical knowledge to the Saxon Settlement, and the second when Group II boys groped for explanations of the behaviour of the physics apparatus. At best, the two processes go on at once; the new knowledge helps them to find new meanings in the old experience, and finding words for the old helps them see the application of the new. In the group discussions there were just occasional hints of this reciprocal influence, such as when Group III related their own experience of older people to the woman in the poem, or when one boy in Group II saw a relationship between blowing across pieces of paper and the air flowing over an aircraft's wing. In any real learning it is not just a matter of adding new knowledge: what we 'know already' becomes changed, just as Group III 'saw' the picture of the Saxon village differently after they had discussed the settlers' problems.

Beyond this there is a further kind of learning, when a learner by trying to impose his purposes on the world learns thereby more about the world, and also about his purposes. This did not occur in the groups, though Group II came nearest to such learning when they manipulated the science apparatus to answer questions of their own. Some teachers believe that adolescents should be encouraged to try to change the conditions of their own lives and those of the community which they live in. Indeed, if they engage in sustained effort to organize public action about (for example) bus services, or even to change school rules, they may come to perceive differently the processes of social control, and their own share in them. This would create action knowledge, though it would not necessarily have been codified and reflected upon. In this case the new knowledge would not have been transmitted by the school; the pupils might far outrun their mentors. What they learnt might be very valuable, or might be misleading, or might be evil; action knowledge need not be either good or true. But if school knowledge never becomes action knowledge it is no more than a ticket to higher status – and for many adolescents a ticket which they will soon find to be invalid.

It will be clear to the reader that I have been presenting a version of 'knowing' which is very different from tick or cross, know or not-know, rote learning. The journey from being able to parrot a phrase from teacher or book, or imitate a process, or carry out a calculation, to being able to use the idea or the process to solve new problems in new areas is a long one. As Bruner says, an important part of this is turning around on our own traces and telling ourselves what we know. Teachers have become so habituated to thinking of language in terms of communication that many have ceased to consider that it also performs important subjective functions, since it is the major means by which we consciously organize experience and reflect upon it. If in the classroom we limit spoken language to the teacher telling and the pupil replying to cross-examination, and limit written language to getting information from a book and writing it down to show the teacher that the work is done, we ignore and reject the function of speech and writing as an instrument for reshaping experience, that is, as a means of learning. This is why I have emphasized that through language children can come to terms with new knowledge and relate it to what they already know. But this takes time: children need time to assimilate what they are learning by talking and writing about it *in relation to what they know already*. Too many classroom discussions and writing assignments ask children to relate strange information only to other strange information: the conversation is carried out in terms of what the teacher knows, while the child's other experience – in and out of school – is excluded. This prevents the children from engaging in significant recoding of their experience.

2. What Did They Learn in the Groups?

It would be misleading to treat 'knowledge' as if all kinds were alike. Let us now consider the three tasks – scientific, literary, and historical – which were set to these children, and ask ourselves what mental activities were being demanded of them. In what sense would 'recoding' in language be likely to contribute to each kind of knowledge?

In the case of the Saxon Settlement there can be no doubt of the appropriateness of the idea of recoding. The children had already been given a great deal of information about the topic, and had more information to hand in a book. Moreover they possessed out-of-school knowledge – about uncleared land, for example – which was relevant. The task before them was to re-shape this heterogeneous information so that hypotheses could be drawn up from it about the Saxons' likely behaviour. We can see what this reshaping implies by considering one or two failures. In this extract a teacher is present; he is directing Group III's attention back to the sketch as a source of evidence:

Teacher	Does the picture help you at all ... give you any idea of what would have to be done really?
17. P	You'd start farming.
18.	Yes.
19. P	You'd start ploughing fields.
Teacher	What? Just like that ... It's easily said but I ... It's not so easily done just to start farming ... You've said that they'd clear a lot of the wood ... for building. They'd also ...

It is quite clear here that although in some sense or other these girls probably 'knew' that much of the land at that time would be uncleared they are failing to bring this to bear upon the task in hand. What the group required was a preliminary discussion of what the countryside would be like. This would animate the pupils' latent knowledge about pioneers and clearing land, so that it would be available at appropriate points in discussing the Saxons. This kind of reorganizing and re-interpreting can certainly go on best when pupils are required to discuss things for themselves, though this does require the teacher to predict in advance the likelihood of failures of imagination.

Of course, history teaching is not just a matter of bringing latent knowledge to life. Richard in Group IV said: 'And I'd build a moat as well . . . and use a stockade to prevent . . . savages and . . . wolves and bears getting in at you.' His imaginary landscape was well-peopled, but somewhat indiscriminately. Here there is a need for more stories, pictures, descriptions: Richard and the other members of Group IV might then be given a task which would require them in discussion to draw information from the stories, pictures and descriptions. The problem for this history teacher lies in the distance of his sources from the everyday world of his pupils. Books, pictures, even visits to museums and buildings, need a great deal of discussion in order to enable the pupils to interpret what they see and incorporate it into their view of the past. As we saw with Group III, it is quite possible to look at a picture and see nothing in it at all, until you have begun to ask yourself questions about it.

Something very similar happened in the apparatus work on air. When the Group I girls blew between the dangling apples they said no more than:

19. C   They start swinging.
20. T   Yer, they just swing a bit.

Group III were even more emphatic in insisting that *nothing* happened when they blew, and both groups were happy to leave it at that. It seems that unless one has well-formed expectations about what will happen one may fail to perceive what does happen. That is, our perception is partly shaped by our expectations, our interpretation of the situation. In this case it seems likely that the girls would have seen more if they had been asked first to guess what would happen. This is another way in which verbalizing can play a part in learning, by alerting our perceptual expectations.

If the pupils feel no sympathetic interest in the topic and therefore reject it, there can be no effective learning of the kind being discussed. I have already referred to the passage in which Group I girls reject the poem.

10. T	She'd be very childish and go around pressing alarm bells, and . . .
11. C	Things like children do.
12. T	Do yes . . . gobble up samples in the shops. It's all childish.

What they say is perfectly true: at one level they understand the poem perfectly. But their cold withdrawal of sympathy means that they cannot learn from it. Only by an act of sympathy can they bring the poem and their own lives into relation with one another, in order to gain insight into the possibilities of self-repression which the poem presents.

Once again we find, as with air and the Saxon settlement, that the kind of learning which can go on in the groups is a matter of using language on the one hand to animate and reshape existing knowledge, and on the other to try out new knowledge as a way of re-interpreting the old. The extracts we have examined in this section suggest that this emphasis upon talking for learning should be qualified in two ways. First, pupils may need help in verbalizing relevant aspects of what they already know: they would have gained from talk about the terrain before the history task, and from talk about bicycle tyres and so on before the science task. That is, they may need help in making the bridge between the new knowledge and what they already know in their everyday lives.

The second qualification to be made is that unless pupils are willing to take the risk of some emotional commitment they are unlikely to learn. We have observed this in Group I's approach to the poem; it may well play a part in the relatively unproductive approach by both groups of girls to the science task. (We might ask ourselves: What, in the eyes of working-class girls, is the

survival value of an understanding of physical phenomena?)
Although the groups controlled the details of their dialogue, the
subject-matter and the overall problem had been chosen for them.
They could select sub-topics within it, and also the strategies by
which they approached them. The problems selected in history
and science gave them the support of a framework to operate in.
The choice of the poem was less helpful: there was too wide a
gap between the world of the poem and their own action knowledge for them to make meaningful links between them, so that
they finally rejected the poem as irrelevant and silly. This is every
teacher's dilemma: how can one support pupils with a framework
which does not at the same time constrict their participation?
How can one enable the learner to order his own learning without
abandoning him in a trackless wilderness?

If pupils cannot be persuaded to give their sympathetic interest
to what they are learning, teachers will hardly persuade them to
bring it into relationship with their view of the world about them,
their place in it, and their opportunities for influencing it. We
can hardly select a curriculum on the basis of children's existing
interests; but their *potential* interests constitute a demarcation of
what curriculum is possible.

3. Some Effects of Audience on Learning

John H. Flavell has described in this way the state of mind of a
young child.

His cognitive field-of-vision includes the data thought about but not
the process of thinking itself. Insensitive to the very fact that the way
he construes the data is only one construction among many possible . . .
he can scarcely check for cognitive bias his own view of events . . .
Intellectual egocentrism is fundamentally an inability to take roles . . .[2]

This is a summary of Piaget's views on egocentrism. Several of
Piaget's experiments illustrate what he means by egocentrism.
For example, in an experiment with a model of three mountains

2. Flavell, J. H., *et al.* (1968), *The Development of Role-Taking and
Communication Skills in Children*, Wiley.

of different heights arranged on a triangular plan, he showed that young children cannot imagine the mountains as they would appear to someone looking at them from another direction. An adult, however, would set up a more complex mental representation of them which would enable him to reconstruct in imagination how they would appear from another viewpoint. This is one aspect of what Piaget calls 'decentration', the development of more complex mental representations of the world which reconciles different viewpoints, instead of being bound to one only.

The experiments on role-taking and communication carried out by Flavell and his associates not only bring additional empirical support for Piaget's theory of decentration, but also extend its meaning. Flavell's book is devoted to studies of children's ability to take another person's existing knowledge into consideration when giving him information, an ability which increases with age. For example, in one of the studies children of various ages were asked to explain how to play a simple game with counters on a board to someone who did not know it, and then to explain the same game to a second person who was blindfolded, and therefore unable to see the moves made with the counters. Flavell and his associates were thus able to assess how far the children modified their explanations to take into account the second person's need for additional information. The results of this group of experiments suggested that the ability to take another person's knowledge into account increases at least from seven to sixteen years of age.

In Flavell's work decentration is concerned with adopting another person's 'point of view' metaphorically, not literally as with Piaget's mountains experiment. It seems to involve a means of representing to oneself how the other person's knowledge differs from one's own, and thus presents the intersection of social learning with cognition. Decentration may in part be influenced by social processes. The need to collaborate with other people, or to persuade them to adopt one's point of view, will encourage and reward children's attempts to acknowledge other people's viewpoints. Flavell's experiments seemed to require relatively simple cognitive processes. In explaining the game to the blindfolded man it was necessary to remember that 'Next you put that there' would not serve, that all visual information must be put into words. The task, which even older children found quite difficult, required the children *to stand outside their own knowledge and see it as relative.* This suggests that communication plays a part in children's development towards the hypothetico-deductive thinking which Piaget calls Formal Operations.

The groups discussed in the previous chapter seemed to reach hypothetical thinking partly with the aid of manipulable data and partly in order to convey their understanding to one another. It seems possible that in our attempts to say things clearly to other people we progressively learn to build their viewpoints into our own, and thus to see our knowledge (or perceptions) as hypothetical and open to change. As Inhelder and Piaget, comparing young children with adolescents, put it, 'The child has no powers of reflection – i.e. no second-order thoughts which deal critically with his own thinking. No theory can be built without such reflection.'[3] It seems likely that it is the need to communicate with others which gradually lays down during later childhood and adolescence the alternative groundwork from which the child can reflect upon his own thinking. Seventy years ago G. H. Mead expressed a similar idea when in his lectures he said:

I know of no way in which intelligence or mind could arise ... other than through the internalization by the individual of social processes of experience and behavior ... as made possible by the individual's taking the attitudes of other individuals toward himself and toward what is being thought about.[4]

James Moffett has suggested (following Mead's line of thought) that our ability to think depends on the many previous dialogues which we have taken part in. In dialogue speakers take up statements that have gone before and develop them: one adds a qualifying condition, another suggests a cause or a result, another negates the whole statement, another reformulates it, and another qualifies one of the objects which it refers to. As I have shown

3. Inhelder, B. and Piaget, J. (1958), *The Growth of Logical Thinking from Childhood to Adolescence,* Routledge & Kegan Paul.
4. Mead, G. H. (1934), *Mind, Self and Society,* University of Chicago Press.

on p. 44, such a dialogue can be synthesized into a complex cognitive structure. Out of many such discussions (says Moffett) comes the ability to think unsupported by the other participants in dialogue. 'I am asking the reader', he says, 'to associate dialogue with dialectic. The internal conversation we call thinking recapitulates previous utterances *as amended and expatiated on.*' Of the relationship of this to language he writes:

Constructions of time, place and manner are born of when, where and how questions motivated by the listener's desire to get more information from his speaker. The true *because* is born of *why.* The creation of relative clauses and the insertion of interpretative 'signal words' like *however, moreover,* and *therefore* stem from a felt need to relate statements for the benefit of the listener.[5]

It is not that our ability to think waits upon our knowledge of language – Hermine Sinclair de Zwart[6] has shown this to be unlikely – but that the desire to communicate with others plays a dynamic part in the organizing of knowledge.

To summarize: the human mind develops through a process of decentration, in which the child by incorporating alternative viewpoints into his own knowledge develops models of the physical and social world which transcend his original more egocentric viewpoint. Eventually the adolescent is able to approach problems hypothetically since he can (at least potentially) see any interpretation of reality as open to change. This decentration comes in part from the need to communicate with other people, since it necessitates insight into their understanding of the world.

How does this relate to classroom learning? Much of the knowledge which is presented to children in schools requires them to accommodate views of the world which differ from their everyday understandings. For example, I shall discuss in Chapter Four a geography lesson in which pupils who understand the value of goods in terms of their use to a consumer are faced by

5. Moffett, J. (1968), *Teaching the Universe of Discourse,* Houghton Mifflin.
6. Sinclair de Zwart, H., 'Developmental Psycholinguistics' in D. Elkind and J. H. Flavell (eds.) (1969), *Studies in Cognitive Development,* Oxford University Press, N.Y.

a teacher who is talking about their value in terms of profit or loss to a shopkeeper. If these children are to make sense of this contradiction they must (i) make their original assumptions about value explicit to themselves, (ii) listen to what the teacher says, (iii) test their understanding of the teacher's viewpoint in discussion with him, and (iv) make explicit the relationship between consumer and producer, which alone can reconcile the two interpretations. The process which I have just sketched, however, implies that the learners not only receive messages from the teacher but also articulate their own understandings. The two viewpoints cannot be synthesized unless the learners too are engaged in formulating knowledge. What is in question is whether schools do in fact challenge pupils to communicate *their* viewpoints so that they are available to other people with different assumptions. The need to explain to someone who does not understand is crucial. What audiences *are* offered to pupils for their talk and writing? In the passage which follows, Harold Rosen discusses a crucial aspect of the communication system, the role of the teacher as audience, and the effect of this upon pupils' writing.[7]

In school, it is almost always the teacher who initiates the writing and who does so by defining a writing task with more or less explicitness. Not only does he define the task but also nominates himself as audience. He is not, however, simply a one-man audience but also the sole arbiter, appraiser, grader and judge of the performance. He becomes an audience on whom pupils must focus a special kind of scrutiny in order to detect what they must do to satisfy him. The peculiar feature of this relationship is that the pupil will see his teacher's response as a means by which his progress is being charted. It is part of a larger and more elaborate system of making judgements and not simply a question of the reader's pleasure or understanding or insight. Indeed the writer is frequently placed in a position of telling the reader what he already knows more fully and more deeply.

The fact that the pupil is subject to frequent demands for writing, some of which he finds distasteful or merely dull may lead to his sense of audience taking on a particular complexion. His writing may be dominated by the sole consideration of meeting *minimum* requirements.

7. Rosen, H. (1973), 'Written Language and the Sense of Audience', *Educational Research* 15:3, June 1973.

In other words it is shaped solely by the demands of his audience and not by the complementary pressure to formulate in a way which satisfies the writer.

The members of the Writing Research Unit, of whom Dr Rosen is one, have demonstrated that a very large proportion of the writing done in secondary schools is of this kind.

What is likely to be the effect on learning of the teacher as sole audience? A study by Robert Zajonc[8] throws some light on this. He gave two groups of adults a letter to read quickly. He then told one group that they would be describing the character of the letter-writer to a group of people who had not seen the letter. The other group were told that they would be informed of the character of the letter-writer by someone who knew him well. Both groups were given a number of questions to answer about the letter-writer's character. Zajonc found that those who expected to communicate to people who had no prior knowledge wrote quite different answers from those who expected to receive an authoritative answer from elsewhere. Those in the position of authority with respect to the knowledge differentiated the writer's characteristics more sharply, had a more complex view of him, and yet had gone further in unifying and organizing this view. Those expecting to receive an authoritative opinion had stored a much vaguer and less organized view of the writer. This experiment suggests that when we know that we are going to have to tell someone else, we begin long before to organize and shape the knowledge. Thus a teacher is likely to be a poor audience for pupils' speech and writing: if they believe him to possess authoritative knowledge, pupils will be less likely to order their thoughts for him than they would for an uninformed audience.

Flavell, who refers to this study by Zajonc, also describes an unpublished experiment by Kraus and Glucksber (1965) in which children described shapes to be identified by other children who could not see them. They established incidentally that even when young children's descriptions failed to communicate they enabled the children themselves to identify the shapes weeks later. The attempt to code the shapes for another child had influenced the

8. Zajonc, R. B. (1960), 'The Process of Cognitive Tuning in Communication', *Journal of Abnormal and Social Psychology*, Vol. 61.

manner in which they themselves had coded and stored the information.

In Chapter Two I was able to show in some detail how Glyn's success in formulating acceptable explanations depended to a considerable degree upon Steve. This was partly a matter of Steve's questioning, but it is now clear that the whole of Steve's role as interested layman will have contributed by encouraging Glyn to be more explicit. In traditional teacher-class discussions the teacher's academic authority will thus *tend to inhibit many children's active reshaping of knowledge.* Similarly with writing, when it is of the kind described by Rosen. This is less likely to be true when a pupil is explaining some matter about which he knows more than the teacher, or when he is talking or writing for another audience. But neither of these often happen, for most teachers firmly control the knowledge which is dealt with in their lessons and exclude as irrelevant those matters for which they cannot claim competence.

There would seem to be good reason for teachers to experiment with alternative patterns of communication which would offer a variety of audiences for their pupils' talk and writing, some of which would give to pupils authoritative control of the knowledge. My discussion of small groups in the previous chapter was intended to suggest that this is one communication pattern which can generate different learning strategies. (I have included in the Appendix some suggestions of ways of increasing pupils' control without leaving them unsupported.) James Britton and his colleagues of the Writing Research Unit have experimented with written work addressed to the writer's peers, and audiences for writing beyond the confines of school can often be devised.

The tape-recorder too offers to teachers the possibility of finding a wider range of audiences for their pupils' spoken language. Thirteen-year-olds are not necessarily able to imagine what it is that an audience needs to be told, and how they need to shape a message for different audiences. It would therefore be necessary to help them to become more aware of the needs of more distant audiences, for modifying knowledge for others can enable the pupils themselves to see it differently. Glyn and Steve were exceptionally aware of the presence of the tape-recorder, and especially aware that they had to be explicit because their future audience would not be able to see the apparatus and how they were using it. Here they are repeating the task of blowing between dangling apples.

48. S		Yes, hold on, let's start again . . . I'll do it the first this time. [Blowing] Oh! they hit together.
49. G		'Cos you blow all the pressure away from inside and the pressure outside knocks 'em together.
50. S		Oh! Tell that into the microphone.
51. G		That . . . [inaudible] . . . there.
52. S		When you blow the two apples you brought [it] together, this is because . . . go! [whisper]
53. G		Because you're knocking all the pressure out of the middle of the apples . . . and then the . . . er . . . pressure on the other side of the apples forces them together.

It is Steve who is aware of the demands of the recording. Glyn is at first so daunted by it as to be unable to enunciate clearly. Steve translates Glyn's relatively inexplicit reference to the apples ('knocks 'em together') into 'the two apples', and takes on the task of presenting Glyn in the role of explainer: 'This is because . . . go!', and this leads to progress in the explicit analysis of the process.

The effect of Steve's reminders on the explicitness of Glyn's explanations suggests that for pupils capable of imagining an absent audience the tape-recorder would offer an alternative means of reporting back. Such a recorded report might be available to the teacher, to other pupils in various classes, and to visitors. Moreover, the tape-recorder can be used as a means of increasing pupils' ability to reshape knowledge for others. For example, a group can play the recording back to themselves later to discover where they have not been explicit enough. At a later stage, recorded reports would offer a basis for further study of the topic, such as a discussion of what should be included in written 'notes', or of the pro's and con's of different ways of phrasing an explanation. It is by such means as these that pupils can learn to understand an area of knowledge more deeply in the course of preparing it for a wider audience. (Many a teacher has said that he did not fully understand some part of his subject until he came to teach it.) This is the business of all teachers, and not only English specialists: the organization of language necessitates the organization of thought – except when speech or writing becomes no more than a means of satisfying the teacher.

This does however require an important qualification. Using language to explain ideas to an unknown audience is very different from using language to organize ideas for ourselves (or for a small group of intimates). Teachers should be careful to avoid by-passing the exploratory stage, by expecting pupils to spell out for outsiders something they are only beginning to make sense of. This is why it is necessary to qualify the suggestion made above about the use of the tape-recorder as a means of publication; used prematurely it would 'close' discussion, as it did for Group IV.

No teacher can afford to ignore the influence of social context upon learning – or, in terms of the central concepts of this book, the influence of communication on curriculum. That is why I have devoted this section to the audience for children's speech and writing, a matter which most teachers never give a thought to. Schoolchildren learn to cope with school as best they can; as John Holt has shown, some of what they learn (such as their methods of avoiding having to answer questions) are educationally unproductive. They read from their teacher's voice and face what is expected of them; it is every teacher's business to see to it that the messages they read contribute to learning, not inhibit it. Speech and writing cannot be left for the English lesson; for they affect the learning that goes on throughout the day.

4. Speech and Problem-Solving

It might be argued that although I have shown that adolescents can manipulate and re-interpret their knowledge during discussion this does not necessarily help them to solve problems. Psychologists who have investigated the relationship between speech and cognitive processes have tended to choose mental activities very unlike those which the four groups undertook. There is a multitude of published studies relating to the effect of naming or describing upon perception, discrimination, recognition, or memory, but these are only marginally relevant to the matter in hand. The Russian psychologist Luria[9] reports an impressive series of experiments intended to show that as children mature from two to five years of age they become progressively more able to control their actions by speech, first audible and then inner speech. (Attempts to replicate Luria's experiments have however met with mixed results so the matter is still open to debate.[10]) There are however a few studies which approach directly the effect of speech upon problem-solving.

Gagné and Smith[11] set the adolescent boys who were their subjects a series of problems which required them to move a pile of discs according to rules which governed the moves which they could make. The earlier problems of the series could be solved by random moves, but in the later problems those who grasped the underlying principle would find the solution in fewer moves. Thus subjects who completed the task in fewer moves would be those who had grasped the principle. Half of the subjects were asked to explain as they made a move why they were doing it, and these were significantly more successful in solving the problems. It seemed that explaining the purpose of their moves helped the subjects to re-interpret the data in the light of the problem.

In another study, M. R. Marks[12] gave adults the task of finding out where in the course of a computation a group of errors had occurred. There were four possible sources of error to be investigated. In the part of the experiment which concerns us here, Marks placed in front of some of his subjects a written list of possible sources of error but this had no effect upon their success. However, he interrupted some subjects at intervals in order to

9. Luria, A. R. (1959), 'The Directive Function of Speech in Development and Dissolution', in R. C. Oldfield and J. C. Marshall (eds.), *Language: Selected Readings*, Penguin (1968).

10. Referred to in Cazden, C. B. (1972), *Child Language and Education*, Holt, Rinehart & Winston.

11. Gagné, R. M., and Smith, E. C. (1962), 'A Study of the Effects of Verbalisation on Problem Solving', *Journal of Experimental Psychology* Vol. 63, pp. 12–18.

12. Marks, M. R. (1951), 'Problem Solving as a Function of the Situation', *Journal of Experimental Psychology* Vol. 41, pp. 74–80.

ask them to put into words the ways in which the errors could have occurred. This group proved very much more likely to reach a correct solution than those who were presented with a written list or those who received neither the list nor the demands to verbalize one for themselves. It is worth noticing that this part of the experiment included not only verbalizing but also a face-to-face relationship in which the experimenter's questions played an important part, since like the questions of a skilful teacher they required the learner to represent to himself what he already knew. It was necessary for the subjects themselves to talk about possibilities: someone else's list did not help them to solve the problem.

Speech, while not identical with thought, provides a means of reflecting upon thought processes, and controlling them. Language allows one to consider not only what one knows but how one knows it, to consider, that is, the strategies by which one is manipulating the knowledge, and therefore to match the strategies more closely to the problem. This view is supported by Lunzer[13] who describes a study of children's problem-solving carried out by his associate Astin. As one would expect, the number of moves needed to solve a given problem decreased with the children's ages (four to ten years). However, at about seven or eight years of age most children suddenly became able to reverse the test and set it to the experimenter; at much the same time the children became able to explain their solution of the test. Lunzer argues that in order to 'reverse' the test it was not enough for the child to be able to represent his own actions to himself; he needed to be able to represent the criteria on which these actions were chosen and ordered. The ability to verbalize principles and the ability to reverse a process by playing the role of the other may thus be closely related – related by identity rather than by cause and effect, that is.

Taken together, these studies suggest that learners will achieve more insight into underlying principles (i) if they themselves rehearse aloud the demands of the task which they are facing; (ii) if they put into words what they are doing with the data, and with what purpose; (iii) if they do so repeatedly in response to

13. Lunzer, E. A. (1968), *The Regulation of Behaviour*, Staples Press.

questions from someone else. Unfortunately none of these experimenters provided a detailed analysis of the language used by their subjects, though this might have proved most informative.

Many of the reasoning tasks which children face in school will differ from those used by the experimenter in that they will not be well-formed. A problem is well-formed if (like an arithmetical calculation) it is open to a single solution, the validity of which can be demonstrated. The Saxon settlements task was far from well-formed: many different answers could be defended as reasonable. The poem was similarly open to a range of acceptable interpretations. (I am not saying that the range is infinite.) The air pressure task presented an intermediate case. If the pupils had been asked to measure changes in air pressure this would have been closer to a well-formed problem, whereas the demand to *explain* will never give a well-formed task unless the criteria for an acceptable explanation have been agreed upon in advance. It will be clear to the reader that most of the choices we make in everyday life are not solutions to well-formed problems but are more like the tasks presented to the groups.

If children in school are faced with well-formed problems this is likely to be in mathematics or the physical sciences. (We must remember too that what is a well-formed problem to the teacher who sets it may not be well-formed to the pupil who receives it, if he has not grasped the system in terms of which the problem has been formulated.) The Saxon settlements is typical of the majority of those school learning tasks which go beyond memorizing. Tasks of this kind compel the pupil to *decide on what principles the data will be selected and ordered*, whereas in a well-formed problem this is already decided. In effect, the children when they discussed the Saxon settlements had to formulate problems as well as offer solutions. Speech is likely to have a more complex part to play in learning of this kind than it had in the three experimental studies which I have referred to. We can predict, however, from the study carried out by Marks, that with tasks like Saxon settlements the interpretations put into words by the pupils themselves are likely to have much more effect in reorganizing their knowledge than would interpretations spoken to them by someone else.

5. Reflexivity: The Learner's Control of Knowledge

For some readers the view of knowledge which I have been presenting will be a familiar one, easily related for example to Piaget's views. For others it may seem contrary to common sense. Many teachers see knowledge as the possession of trained adults, who have achieved it through years of study of a discipline. The idea of thirteen-year-olds making knowledge will seem nonsense from this point of view: the laws of physics are there to be discovered, not invented. I do not wish to dismiss this view out of hand. (Chapter Five will include a study of the different views of knowledge held by a sample of secondary school teachers.)

I write of thirteen-year-olds 'making knowledge' because even when a trained physicist has formulated in words or other symbols a series of statements which describe (say) how liquids behave under pressure, these statements may be useless to other people. They remain no more than marks upon paper until the learners have worked upon it themselves, and related it to what they already know. Every state of knowledge is achieved by a re-ordering of the state of knowledge that preceded it: this view of knowledge dates back at least to Hegel's writings.

More recently, the idea of language as a tool for making meaning as well as for communicating existing meanings was very clearly present in the writings of the anthropologist Edward Sapir, who wrote:

Once the form of a language is established it can discover meanings for its speakers which are not simply traceable to the given quality of experience itself but must be explained to a large extent as the projection of potential meanings into the raw material of experience.[14]

Sapir is here crediting this power of generating new meanings not to the language as a whole but to speech, which is what men do with language. A similar view has been held by more than one school of psychologists. The Russian psychologist L. S. Vygotsky

14. Sapir, E. (1949), *Selected Writings in Language, Culture and Peronsality*, University of California Press.

in his influential book *Thought and Language*, written in the early thirties, presents speech as a means of guiding action and interpreting the world.

Speech for oneself originates through differentiation from speech for others . . . It does not merely accompany the child's activity; it serves mental orientation, conscious understanding; it helps in overcoming difficulties . . .[15]

The American psychologist Jerome Bruner has consistently urged the importance of language in cognitive development. He extends this importance to the act of speaking when he describes language as: 'not only the medium of exchange but the instrument the learner can use himself in bringing order into the environment'.[16] There is an important difference between arguing that the development of cognition depends on the development of language – an assertion which Piaget has firmly rejected – and arguing that speech enables us to control thought. It is the second of these which is at the heart of this book. Sapir, Vygotsky and Bruner hold this in common: they all see language both as a means by which we learn to take part in the life of the communities we belong to, and a means by which we can actively reinterpret the world about us, including that life itself. Through language we both *receive* a meaningful world from others, and at the same time *make meanings* by re-interpreting that world to our own ends.

A view of the social functions of reflexivity is put forward in this passage by Jenny Cook-Gumperz.

Through members' talk [members of society, that is] the continuing social scene is made visible to the participants and becomes the subject of their reflexive control. Members' abilities to reflect cognitively and linguistically upon the present stream of events and thoughts enable them to look for and to make social orders in their daily behaviour. In this way men acquire the ability given in the quotation from Schütz . . . to '*work not only within but upon the world*'. Society

15. Vygotsky, L. S. (1962) *Thought and Language*, Massachusetts Institute of Technology Press.

16. Bruner, J. S. (1966), *Toward a Theory of Instruction*, Belknap Press, Harvard.

becomes not an enforced constraint upon men, but men's production and accomplishment.[17]

This implicitly acknowledges that culture includes much that is not readily available to reflection. Language makes reflection possible because it enables us to represent our understandings to ourselves so that we can see them as open to modification in the light of our larger purposes. We are able to withstand the pain of medical treatment because we are able to interpret it as finally beneficial: an animal would fight to escape.

Of course we do not always reflect upon experience when we speak: for the most part what we say to one another carries lightly the common assumptions upon which normal life depends. It may be salutary for every teacher to reflect occasionally upon the tone of voice and vocabulary with which he tells a pupil to carry on with his work: if he reflected thus upon everything he said, teaching would cease. Sometimes we use language to prevent ourselves from knowing something we do not wish to know. Men have the ability to reflect upon what they say; this does not imply that they always do so, or always should do so.

6. Action, Reflexivity and the Stranger

Alfred Schütz, in a paper called 'The Stranger',[18] points out that we do not hold all of our knowledge alike: some we can easily reflect upon and modify, but much of our knowledge is so deeply embedded in our way of coping with life that we don't know that we know it. Schütz uses the stranger who visits another country to illustrate this. As soon as he tries to take part in the life about him he finds that he is no longer able to influence people or to detect what underlies what they say or do. Even if he knows the language well, he is at a loss to understand the meanings which lie beneath the explicit messages. Schütz says that in order to

17. Cook-Gumperz, J. (1973), *Social Control and Socialisation*, Routledge & Kegan Paul.
18. Schütz, A., 'The Stranger: An Essay in Social Psychology', reprinted in *School and Society: A Sociological Reader*, Routledge & Kegan Paul (1971).

understand the implicit beliefs that underlie everyday life in the new culture, the stranger will be compelled not only to understand *them* but will have to bring out for conscious reflection much of the implicit knowledge on which his former life was based. Schütz's message is that we achieve reflexive awareness when we try to *act upon someone whose implicit beliefs are different from our own.*

Thus Schütz sees our knowledge to be arranged in what he calls 'contour lines of relevance'. At the centre is the highly reflexive knowledge, which we are aware of because we have to sustain ånd use it in a world of people with conflicting views. Further out, the contour lines mark areas of knowledge and belief which are less and less open to introspection, until at the periphery lie those areas of assumptions about reality – such as belief in the permanence of objects – which we act on every day but hardly ever bring to mind. Our ability to live normal lives is entirely dependent upon these elaborate systems of tacit knowledge. 'The stranger' may have to bring parts of this tacit knowledge into full focus if he is to become an active participant in the country he has visited.

Maxine Greene,[19] summarizing another paper by Schütz, writes that the learner's 'focal concern is with ordering the materials of his own life world when dislocations occur, when what was once familiar abruptly appears strange'. This reminds one of Piaget: the learner who actively recodes his perceptions when faced with discontinuity or contradiction matches Piaget's concept of 'accommodation'. But Piaget too has emphasized that we can hold knowledge with different degrees of awareness, different degrees of reflexivity: it is reflexivity which makes possible the hypothetico-deductive thinking which marks off formal operations from the earlier stages of cognitive development. Formal operations arise when we become capable of thinking about thinking, and are thus able to take responsibility for the strategies we use.

This line of thought raises the possibility that it is the 'stranger' experience which leads to the development of hypothetical and

19. Greene, M. (1971), 'Curriculum and Consciousness', *Teachers College Record*, 73:2, p. 253.

reflexive forms of thinking. Are formal operations the typical mental approaches of marginal man who belongs neither to the culture he has left nor the one he aspires to? Is this why in some cultures – and perhaps in some sub-cultures – people achieve formal operations later than in others, and may not achieve them at all? Something similar is implicit in Bernstein's theory too; some families protect their children from 'the stranger' experience and thus delay their movement towards reflexive thinking.

Education – at least in western urban cultures – seems almost to be designed to promote in children a long series of 'stranger' experiences. The child is placed in situations where because of the teacher's control he can only gain approval by intuiting the 'rules' of the classroom subculture. Most learn to fit in with the social demands made on them, but there are cognitive demands also. As soon as a child seems to have achieved an acceptable academic performance, a new system of knowledge is opened up; behind every achieved understanding is a door to a re-interpretation which modifies the first. The successful pupil has to cope with these perpetually revised demands which draw him forever onwards; no sooner has one reality been grasped than another appears, and at secondary school level these become multiple. These progressive denials of the child's existing knowledge force him towards 'the stranger's' self-awareness: he meets each teacher and each teacher's way of thinking like a stranger who tries to reconstruct the implicit rules of another culture. Those who fail fall back on the certainties of home and peer group, and cease to try to comprehend the shifting realities projected by the school. In this way, our education seems to be designed to force children towards formal operations.

Margaret Mead[20] contrasts education in Melanesian and European cultures. In many non-industrialized cultures there are no educational institutions: children learn by living and working with older relatives who make it their business to involve them actively so that they acquire necessary skills and information.

20. Mead, M. (1942), 'Our Educational Emphases in Primitive Perspective', reprinted in *Tinker, Tailor* . . . N. Keddie (ed.) (1973), Penguin. Much of the thinking in this section has been provoked by the papers collected by Miss Keddie in that volume.

The usefulness of the learning is patent to the learner, since he is contributing to the means of life of his group; the learning arises from 'making sense of his life world'. For European children much of their learning goes on in schools, which are in their intrinsic nature separate from the practical concerns of adult members of the culture. (When children write in school, for example, they seldom write real messages but merely 'practice writing'.) The 'life world' of a European child may seem very distant from the school, except for those who see the tasks set by the school to be at the centre of their life world, that is, see them to be the means by which they can control their futures. A European child is not only required to find his way into 'a structure of socially prescribed knowledge' which may have little obvious relevance to his life world, but when he has made sense of it he will be presented with yet another structure lying beyond it.

This way of presenting the matter goes too far towards presenting European children as passive victims of their cognitive marginality, forever reaching towards an intellectual security which eludes their grasp. Maxine Greene supplies a counterbalance to this: 'We pay too little attention to the individual in quest of his own future, bent on surpassing what is merely "given", on breaking through the everyday.' One of my themes in this book has been precisely this; the detailed examination of the group discussions in Chapter Two was intended to illustrate that children *can themselves break through the everyday* even when grappling with tasks which a teacher has given them, and which may therefore not play a central part in their life worlds.

It is when we try to act upon and with our fellows that we discover whether we inhabit the same universe with them. But these actions must arise out of our own purposes, out of our will to shape the world to our own ends. This is why Schütz's idea of the child's 'life world' is important, since it is out of this that his purposes will arise. Freire, in *The Pedagogy of the Oppressed*, urges his peasants into political action to achieve their immediate ends, since only such action will enable them to make conscious their background awareness of their own plight. Action will lead them to recode their own experience so that in the end action and learning become one. Most formal education is empty of such action, however full it may be of doing things. It is not a question of 'relevance', or 'irrelevance' but of 'my purposes' and 'other people's purposes'. When the teacher's purposes are as arbitrary as they sometimes appear, the pupils' subordination to them is potentially alienating.

Learning can be a passive acceptance of the beliefs and practices of the people about us; in our culture however we have learnt to value reflexive thought, the knowledge which we ourselves can shape and reapply. Reflexive learning seems to occur when a learner, acting upon purposes which are significant in his life world, is faced with disjunction between his implicit beliefs and those of the persons he is interacting with. This disjunction compels him, if he is to continue his purposed action, to bring to sharp awareness parts of his world which were upon the periphery of his consciousness, and to construct for himself understandings which did not previously exist. If he has a teacher he will learn by open confrontation with the teacher's life world; each will learn from trying to represent the other's style of understanding. But this will only happen if both teacher's and learner's purposes are engaged; the alternative is a ritual transmission and assessment directed towards examinations and not towards action. Learning from disjunction can be generated by two equals, such as Glyn and Steve, if they trust one another sufficiently to work towards mutual understanding, and if they find subject-matter which falls within the range of their purposes. Finally it is not impossible to learn thus alone, for example in the kind of writing in which one is implicitly qualifying and shaping what one writes in order to deal with the opinions of an imagined reader, who may be an alternative aspect of oneself, another voice in the internal dialogue.

It is no wonder that most working-class children do themselves less than justice in schools. For many of them the disjunction between the teacher's purposes and their own is great; they are likely to receive less encouragement, if not actual discouragement, from their teachers; finally their families often do not see education as a likely way to advancing their interests, though they may see what it does for others. These are amongst the reasons why, as Nell Keddie points out, lower stream children are less willing to accept uncritically the constraints of the teacher's frame of reference. I am not recommending an education which does not face them with the disjunctions upon which reflexive thought depends, but I am saying that education must co-opt their purposes or the disjunctions will be barriers, not challenges.

Chapter Four
The Teacher's Control of Knowledge

1. Exploratory Speech and Final Draft

In the group discussions presented in Chapter Two it was clear
that many of the children were rearranging their thoughts during
improvised talk. This did not make for explicit communication
but it played an important part in the problem-solving. I called
this use of language 'exploratory'. This is not identical with the
hypothetical mode, though the tentativeness of exploratory talk
may for many children be a necessary condition for achieving
hypothesis forming and testing.

When teachers entered the groups, asking questions intended
to further their pupils' understanding, the style of speech shifted
away from the exploratory towards a style appropriate to showing
the teacher that they had 'the right answer'. The use of exploratory language did not seem to reflect different abilities of particular children but rather the degree of control over knowledge
which they felt themselves to have. They ceased to use language
to shape knowledge for themselves as soon as the authority of
the teacher was present. However, not all speech or writing
addressed to teachers is of the clipped, inexplicit kind used for
example by the girls of Group III. I wish to use the name 'final
draft' for writing – or, less frequently, speech – which amounts
to a formal completed presentation for a teacher's approval.
Final draft language is the contrary of exploratory: far from
accompanying (and displaying) the detours and dead-ends of
thinking, it seeks to exclude them and present a finished article,
well-shaped and polished. Whether writing or speech tends towards the exploratory or towards a final draft will depend upon the
speaker's or writer's interpretation (and awareness) of the audience

he is addressing. In some classrooms the teacher pre-empts the nature of the audience that the children talk or write for.

The manner in which an intimate or a distant audience tends to constrain speech can be illustrated in this highly simplified manner.

	Intimate Audience	Distant Audience
Size	Small group	Full class
Source of authority	The group	The teacher
Relationships	Intimate	Public
Ordering of thought	Inexplicit	Explicit
Speech planning	Improvised	Pre-planned
Speech function	Exploratory	Final draft

A group of children working alone are likely to find exploratory talk available to them if they know one another well. Equal status and mutual trust encourages thinking aloud: one can risk inexplicitness, confusion and dead-ends because one trusts in the tolerance of the others. The others are seen as collaborators in a joint enterprise rather than as competitors for the teacher's approval. Groups I and III at times forgot the tape-recorder enough for this to happen. Group II, though they adopted a hypothetical approach to the science task, were more aware of the recorder and therefore tended to be less exploratory, aiming instead at authoritative statements. Group IV viewed the recorder as a teacher-substitute (which in a way it was) and attempted a final draft style of speaking which they could not sustain.

It will be clear from the previous paragraph that the diagram above is not intended to be deterministic. A group can redefine the nature of its audience and task; so can a teacher for his class. I shall show below how one teacher was able by a careful redirection of her authority to change radically the speech-functions available to pupils in her lessons.

Two American psychologists, Jeanne Watson and Robert Potter, make a distinction which seems to be related to what I have been calling 'open' and 'closed' discussions, or 'exploratory' and 'final draft' functions of language. This is in a paper[1] in which they discuss the ways in which two people who talk to one another at a party can set up their temporary relationships. One of their distinctions involves contrasting *presenting* with *sharing*, though these two must shade off imperceptibly into one another. The idea of someone 'presenting' himself derives from Erving Goffman's use of a dramatic metaphor to describe human communication. Each of us *presents* to others a view of himself as he wants to be seen, but this on-stage presentation conceals behind itself a back-stage world which may be revealed only to intimates, or not at all. As Watson and Potter put it:

Presenting, as we define it, consists of interaction which establishes each participant as a unique and separate identity. It is a process in which the self-boundaries of each participant remain intact, and in which each responds from the outside to a façade offered by the other.

At the other end of the scale we have *sharing*, in which each participant abandons his façade and allows the other behind the scenes: this implies collaboration, and the willingness to take in the other's point of view, rather than holding it at arm's length.

The process of *sharing* . . . is defined as interaction which establishes overlap between the self-systems of the axis partners . . . In a sense, the self of each participant can be described as expanding to include the qualities of the other person.

Watson and Potter associate 'sharing' with willingness to change by entering into the lives and experiences of others, and go on to say that both presenting and sharing have a part to play in the development of the self. If we perceive other people as threatening critics, ready to judge us and show up our inadequacies, we are likely to put on a display, to concentrate on the external acceptability of what we say and do. Such people are likely to influence our behaviour in an external way, whereas people whom we collaborate with in an unthreatening relationship are likely to influence us more deeply since we shall have to achieve sympathetic insight into their view of reality in order to collaborate successfully with them.

1. Watson, J. and Potter, R. J. (1962), 'An Analytic Unit for the Study of Interaction', *Human Relations* 15:2.

This applies with especial force to children in school, since it is teachers who determine what classroom relationships shall be, and exercise power over their pupils. The teacher's traditional task has two aspects which I shall call *Reply* and *Assess*. When a teacher *replies* to his pupils he is by implication taking their view of the subject seriously, even though he may wish to extend and modify it. This strengthens the learner's confidence in actively interpreting the subject-matter; teacher and learner are in a collaborative relationship. When a teacher *assesses* what his pupils say he distances himself from their views, and allies himself with external standards which may implicitly devalue what the learner himself has constructed. Both reply and assess are essential parts of teaching; *assessment* is turned towards the public standards against which pupils must eventually measure themselves, whereas *reply* is turned towards the pupil as he is, and towards his own attempts, however primitive, to make sense of the world.

If a teacher stresses the assessment function at the expense of the reply function, this will urge his pupils towards externally acceptable performances, rather than towards trying to relate new knowledge to old. In this case, the externals of communication – accepted procedures, the vocabulary and style of the subject, even the standard lay-out for writing – are likely to be given more weight than the learner's attempts to formulate meaning. A classroom dialogue in which sharing predominates over presenting, in which the teacher replies rather than assesses, encourages pupils when they talk and write to bring out existing knowledge to be reshaped by new points of view being presented to them. This is likely to be difficult for teacher and pupil alike. As one member of the Humanities Curriculum Project has put it: 'Many teachers ... have been socialized into a tradition of teacher dominance, custodial attitudes and hadn't really known it, because they'd seen themselves as liberals ...'[2] Some pupils too may never see school as anything but threatening. (This may be why Group IV was so defensive.)

2. Macdonald, B. in an interview printed in B. Hamingson (ed.) (1973), *Towards Judgement: The Publication of the Evaluation Unit of the Humanities Curriculum Project*, Centre for Applied Research in Education, University of East Anglia.

We cannot expect exploratory talk or writing when pupils perceive their teacher to be more concerned to assess than to reply. That is, the teacher's habitual responses to what pupils say or write sets up a communication system in which presentation or sharing predominates, and this will affect the kind of learning which goes on.

A very similar distinction is made by Simon and Boyer[3] when they are analysing systems for the description of classroom communication. In dealing with what they call the 'affective domain' of communication they distinguish two dimensions: (i) Support – Non-support, and (ii) Understanding – Judging. The first deals with the expression of negative or positive feeling by the teacher, and includes 'accepts feelings', 'expresses pleasure', 'complains', 'attacks person'. It is the second dimension Understanding – Judging which seems to be identical with Reply – Assess. Simon and Boyer present the dimension thus:

UNDERSTANDING ◄---------- VERSUS ----------► JUDGING

Accepts idea	Positive evaluation ('good')
Clarifies understanding	Negative evaluation ('wrong')
Reflects or paraphrases ideas	Counter proposals, suggestions
Expands on someone else's idea	Implies judgements (should, should never, you always, everybody ought)

They comment:

These categories describe whether a speaker is encouraging a previous speaker to clarify, expand, think through, or tell more about his ideas, or whether he is judging the ideas . . . Positive and negative evaluations are not seen as opposites; they serve, in fact, exactly the same function – that of judging . . . [which] under some circumstances . . . seems to focus attention away from the idea being processed and towards the judgement made.

For my own purposes I would wish also to point out that the 'Understanding' strategy places responsibility in the learner's

3. Simon, A. and Boyer, F. G. (eds.) (1967 and 1970), *Mirrors for Behaviour* (Summary Volume), Research for Better Schools Inc.

hands, reinforcing whatever interpretative framework he is able to contribute, whereas 'Judging' keeps responsibility in the teacher's hands and, even when positive, places the criteria outside the learner's reach.

There appears to be evidence that the teaching tactic which I have called 'Reply' and which Simon and Boyer call 'Understanding' has an effect on learning. Rosenshine[4] summarizes four studies of classroom interaction in which the frequency with which teachers utilized pupils' ideas was correlated with pupils' scores on subsequent tests of subject matter. (Unfortunately he gives no details of the kinds of test used.) 'Utilizing pupils' ideas' included using a pupil's suggestion as the basis for a further step in the argument, comparing it with something already mentioned, or summarizing what several pupils have said. These teaching tactics had more often been related to increases in pupils' scores than had other measures, such as amount of encouragement, or positive versus negative evaluation of what pupils said.

This diagram summarizes the interrelated ideas which I have been presenting in this section; they will be developed further in Chapter Five.

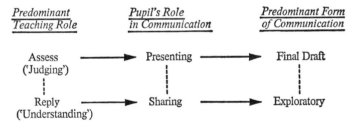

The distinction between exploratory and final draft is essentially a distinction between different ways in which speech can function in the rehearsing of knowledge. In exploratory talk and writing, the learner himself takes responsibility for the adequacy of his thinking; final-draft talk and writing looks towards external criteria and distant, unknown audiences. Both uses of language

4. Rosenshine, B. (1971), 'Teaching Behaviour Related to Pupil Achievement: A Review of Research', in I. Westbury and A. A. Bellack (eds.), *Research into Classroom Processes*, Teachers College Press.

have their place in education. In this book I am emphasizing exploratory language because the social order established in many schools excludes it in favour of final drafts.

Jerome Bruner, so often quoted in these pages, once again supplies a reasoned justification for involving the learner in responsibility for his own learning, presenting the matter through a comparison of a listener's choices with a speaker's choices. In a less well-known paper called 'The Act of Discovery' Bruner made a distinction between:

Two kinds of teaching: that which takes place in the *expository* mode and that in the *hypothetical* mode. In the former the decisions concerning the mode and pace and style of exposition are principally determined by the teacher as expositor; the student is the listener. The speaker has quite a different set of decisions to make: he has a wide choice of alternatives; he is anticipating paragraph content while the listener is still intent upon the words; he is manipulating the content of the material by various transformations while the listener is quite unaware of these internal options. But in the hypothetical mode the teacher and the student are in a more co-operative position with respect to what in linguistics would be called 'speaker's decisions'. The student is not a bench-bound listener, but is taking a part in the formulation and at times may play the principal role in it. He will be aware of alternatives and may even have an 'as if' attitude towards these, and he may evaluate information as it comes.[5]

This distinction between the speaker's choices and the listener's choices seems an important one. It is not that we cannot learn as listeners, but that what we learn is different. When we listen to someone else we can note each step he takes, and 'follow the argument' as the phrase goes, yet without grasping the underlying principles on which the argument has been based. Most of us have had the experience of following a lesson but then finding that we cannot do the exercises on it. When we are placed in the speaker's position we have to have insight into principles in order to construct a step-by-step sequence. It is this grasp of principles, of underlying structures, which makes the difference between rote learning and understanding.

5. Bruner, J. S. (1961), 'The Act of Discovery', reprinted in Bruner, J. S. (1965), *On Knowing: Essays for the Left Hand*, Harvard University Press.

By formulating knowledge for oneself one gains access to the principles on which it is based. In the previous chapter were quoted a number of writers who argued that access to these principles gives one the power to change them. In Geoffrey Esland's phrase, it is the difference between being a 'world-receiver' and a 'world-maker'.[6] The hypothetical mode of learning places responsibility in the learner's hands. The question which will present itself to every teacher is whether children are capable of becoming self-responsible learners. We have seen several groups do so. I have found that given encouraging circumstances even seven- or eight-year-olds can engage in valuable discussion, and this is substantiated by examples collected by Connie Rosen.[7] Nevertheless, every teacher who has used group methods has known occasions when groups wasted time, failed to collaborate, or were frustrated in their attempts to make progress. My contention is that, given appropriately supportive contexts, in the classroom and in the school as a whole, most children can be far more self-responsible learners than most teachers at present allow.

2. What Counts as Knowledge?

From the learner's point of view, language provides a set of strategies for interpreting the world, and a means of reflecting upon this interpretation. Why then is exploratory discussion so infrequent in school lessons? The answer must lie in the social pressures which define what behaviour seems appropriate. These pressures are partly traditional – they constrain the teacher as well as the pupils – but they are under the teacher's control, and therefore open to change.

Pupils' ability to play an active part in the formulation of knowledge is partly controlled by the intentions and expectations

6. Esland, G. M. (1971), 'Teaching and Learning as the Organisation of Knowledge', in M. F. D. Young (ed.) (1971), *Knowledge and Control*, Collier-Macmillan.

7. Rosen, C. and Rosen, H. (1973), *The Language of Primary School Children*, Penguin.

which they bring to lessons, and partly by the patterns of communication set up by the teacher. Harold and Connie Rosen have discussed with useful examples the kind of positive guidance by teachers in primary schools which supports children in understanding their own experience by talking about it. I do not wish to add examples here, but rather to discuss in more general terms some aspects of teachers' behaviour which are likely to limit their pupils' participation in learning, in order to understand why many teachers should feel this to be necessary.

The teacher's control of knowledge can be theoretically distinguished from his control of the social order of the classroom, though much of what teachers do in lessons is concerned with both of these at once. Language performs two functions simultaneously: it carries the message that you are wanting to communicate and at the same time it conveys information about who you think you are, who you think you are talking to, what you believe the situation to be, and so on. Whenever you talk, your speech both carries the conscious message and – usually unconsciously – negotiates the social relationships which you are taking part in. Similarly in schools, whatever is said by teacher or pupil tends to relate both to what is learnt – that is, to the effective curriculum – and to social relationships.

Speech is not only a tool which each of us can use in making sense of the world, but also a means of imposing our version of the world on others. What people about us say and do, if we respond to it at all, is pressing upon us an interpretation of the world and also of ourselves and what we are capable of. In positions of relative powerlessness, such as being a patient in a hospital, or – to a lesser extent – being a pupil in a school, this interpretation may constitute a major source of knowledge about who we are and where we stand.

A recent television programme prepared for the Open University illustrated this admirably.[8] Film sequences followed a senior surgeon in a teaching hospital, accompanied by his juniors and pupils, as he went on his rounds of the wards, first speaking to a patient and then stepping back to discuss his case. The

8. 'Hospital Reality', Course E262, Television Programme No. 2, Open University.

messages and speech-styles addressed to the patients contrasted strikingly with those addressed to the other doctors. In both cases one was aware not only of the channelling of selected information but also of strong pressure to accept a particular definition of situation. The words addressed to the patients implied warmth, calm and sympathy, accepted the patient's uninformed view of himself but gave no information in return. A moment later, when the doctors stepped back to discuss the case – perhaps a possible amputation – their speech switched immediately to a style of ponderous impersonality, full of in-group abbreviations, which served to distance the doctors from the personal reality of the patient and to support their exercise of power. The role of speech in sustaining and separating these two simultaneous but contradictory interpretations of reality could not be more sharply presented. One wonders whether a similar demonstration could be made in a school.

In school, the teacher's and the pupil's views of the world are face to face. The confrontation can only be avoided if the teacher insists on the reality of his knowledge, and rules that the pupils' knowledge is irrelevant. One cannot imagine that many teachers would do this deliberately, though one can sometimes hear a teacher implicitly dismiss a child's existing knowledge by means of phrases such as 'a bad home' or 'deprived' or 'no experience to work on'. It is a matter of interest to discover how it is that children's existing knowledge is often excluded. The key to this lies in the way in which many teachers control both what is discussed, and how it is discussed.

Let us imagine a child who finds that his science teacher cuts him short when, in a lesson about light, he tries to tell an anecdote about shadows. To the teacher the anecdote is irrelevant: he has planned the work with beams of light and prisms in order to present to the pupils the physical principles which he has chosen to teach. For the learner, however, the shadows constitute his starting-point, the source of the understanding which he will bring to the prisms and beams of light. It is understanding of shadows which must be reconstituted to become a grasp of the physical principles. Thus what is irrelevant to the teacher may be very relevant to one of his pupils. The teacher makes decisions about which lines to pursue and which to leave, and these may often save wasted time. But if learners are always discouraged from utilizing the understanding which they do possess they will come to believe that school knowledge is esoteric and unrelated to the practical reasonableness of everyday action knowledge. They will then fail to use what they do know, and make wild guesses when asked a question. Moreover they are likely to undervalue their own ability to think, since they have been shown that what they know already is valueless in school. Much teaching, especially in secondary schools, depends upon generating an artificial dependency in the learners, so that they can gain knowledge only by submitting to the teacher's view and not by thinking for themselves.

Some years ago I saw a lesson which illustrated this all too well. A geography teacher in a rural secondary school had prepared a lesson for his fourth-year mixed-ability class. He distributed copies of an excellent aerial photograph of the area around the school. Most of the pupils came from farms in the area: the photograph reflected their world to them, the patterns of settlement, the communication systems, the distribution of cultivation and pasture. I expected a fine discussion, for the photograph would enable them to reflect upon their everyday knowledge and to see it more schematically. But the teacher wrote three words on the blackboard, 'shape', 'tone', and 'texture', and asked for definitions. In the end he himself had to provide a definition of 'shape'. Then he asked, 'What can you learn from the *shapes* in the photograph about this area?' He was met with silence. By insisting that the pupils talked about the photograph *in his terms* he detached them from what they knew best, their everyday lives. They could not join in the discussion on his terms, and the teacher had prevented them from starting on their terms – which would have enabled him to introduce his own more abstract analytical categories during the discussion. He was asking them to arrive without having travelled, and this is often the effect of demands for final drafts. This anecdote presents an extreme case: few teachers set out so manifestly to devalue their pupils' action knowledge and create artificial dependency on school knowledge. Yet a similar devaluation is often implicit in the language used by teachers, in a lack of interest in the pupil's viewpoint, or in an insistence on the forms of a written report while a pupil is still struggling to make sense of the content.

3. Directing Pupils' Learning: An Example

Elsewhere I have illustrated in detail how a number of secondary teachers, without in the least intending it, constricted the ways in which their pupils were able to participate in lessons,[9] and I should like to direct any sceptical readers to this evidence. Here I shall present only one example, though a lengthy one, which is the opening of a geography lesson taught in a first-year class in a secondary modern school in a rural area. The teacher, a geography specialist, was not a regular teacher of the class though he had taught some of the children in another school. Although much of what I write will seem to criticize this teacher's lesson, I must emphasize that I wish to evaluate the classroom norms within which he was working and not his skills as a teacher. He is a skilled and systematic teacher, kindly and sympathetic to his pupils. While his unfamiliarity with the pupils may have combined with his awareness of the tape-recorder to make him specially eager to control the lesson, this should be balanced against his declared wish to encourage active participation by the pupils. Does an able and experienced teacher who is explicitly committed to encouraging lively discussion succeed in achieving this within the framework of a conventional lesson?

The teacher has planned a lesson on Trade, a topic which has arisen in a previous lesson. He wishes to enable his pupils, a streamed class of eleven-year-olds of average ability, to distinguish between Local Trade, Home Trade, and International Trade. He appears to have planned this sequence for the beginning of the lesson:

1. Define 'Trade'
2. Present the term 'local trade'

9. Barnes, D., Britton, J., and Rosen, H., *Language, the Learner and the School*, Penguin Books, revised edition (1971).

3. Link local trade with perishables
4. Link perishables with threat to profits
5. Present the term 'home trade'

The teacher, after referring to the previous lesson, presents the topic, and elicits a suitable definition of 'trade' by suggesting an inappropriate one.

1. T   Now it was this class . . . that learned something about wheat last time, wasn't it?

2. Ps [several] Yes sir.

3. T   Yes, and we talked also . . . about trade . . . and some of you worked out some . . . trade statistics . . . you . . . drew a graph, I think, one group, on er . . . different countries that spend money on wheat . . . or that exported wheat.

Now to start off with today . . . I want you . . . to . . . think about this word *trade*. [Writing on blackboard] 'Trade . . . and see if you can tell me what is wrong with this . . . thing that I'm going to say. Trade is what you do when you leave school.

4. P   No. No. Trade is where er . . . when you trade summat or you swap something.

5. T   Yes . . . what . . . Is that wrong, what I said? Is it wrong?

6. P   No, there's some trade . . . [inaudible]

7. T   Can you tell me why it's not wrong?

8. P   Er . . . er . . . erm . . . you learn a trade like . . . jo . . . er . . . your father's like joinering, and . . .

9. T   Yes, so that, that word trade does mean something else as well doesn't it? But it means buying and selling to make a profit, in the way that we were using it last time. That's really what it means . . . buying something, and selling it to make a profit. Er . . . does anyone know what a profit is?

10, 11 Ps [two pupils] It means money. Money.

12. T   Yes. Can you be a little more exact than that?

13. P   Well, say you sell some cigarettes for two an . . . you *bought* some cigarettes for two and er . . . six and you sold 'em for two and seven you'd be making a pen . . . penny profit.

14. T   Yes, that's right . . . so it's the money that you make

when you sell something for *more* ... than you paid
for it ... and of course everybody ... every trader ...
is trying to make a profit, isn't he?

Using the local market as his example, the teacher next elicits
from the class examples of perishable goods.

14. T [cont.] Now, I want to think about three different kinds of
trade. The ... the first kind of trade ... perhaps I'd
better write it on the board ... this one ... have we got
a bit of chalk? ... yes here we are ... the first kind of
trade, and I want you to be thinking what this might
mean ... the first kind of trade is called ... [writing]
Local Trade ... now what do you think that means?
This [pointing to *local*] is the clue, isn't it. This is the
clue. What do you think that means? [Child begins to
answer] We've had you once, let's have another.

15. P You sell to people in your own district.

16. T Good lad, yes, that's right. So what goes on at R—
market, on a Thursday, and T— market on a ...
['Monday'–'Wednesday'] ... Monday or a Wednesday,
anyway it'll be on a certain day ... and all these markets
round about ... what goes on there is really local
trade ... and local trade is ... What kind of things,
mostly, will you find in R— market on a Thursday,
shall we say, up at this top end here, nearest to Wool-
worths, along that side? What have, what have most of
the stalls got on them along there?

17. P Vegetables.

18. T Vegetables, anything else?

19. P Fish an ...

20. T Fish ... somebody mentioned another ...

21, 22. Ps [several] Fruit. Fruit.

23. T Fruit ... anything else?

24. P Bacon. Bacon.

25. T Bacon, yes, that's usually a bit further down this side.

26. T Flowers, good lad, yes ... not ... not so much in
winter but in summer you get a lot.

27. P Clothes.

28. T Clothes, they're usually down the other end of the market, aren't they? ['Yes'] ... but they're all there. Now ...
I want you to think about that list of ... list of things

> to sell that we mentioned just now – flowers, vegetables,
> fruit, fish . . .

29. P　　[Quietly] We didn't say fish did we?

Next the teacher elicits that the perishable goods were locally grown.

30. T　　Now these are very often the kind of thing that you
　　　　will find . . . in a local market, trading in your own
　　　　district . . . and . . . what's . . . what's the difference
　　　　between those things, and the other things in the mar-
　　　　ket? Say clothes, and shoes, and Wellington boots . . . ?
　　　　There's a difference straight away.

31. P　　You can't eat . . . shoes.

32. T　　Yes, you can't eat shoes [laughter] . . . and there's
　　　　another difference, which is probably more important.

33. P　　They're made somewhere else.

34. T　　Yes . . . which are?

35. P　　Erm . . . shoes and clothes and . . .

36. T　　Yes, they're made somewhere else and they're brought
　　　　to R— What about the vegetables and the fruit and
　　　　things?

37. P　　You can eat fruit and you can't eat shoes.

38. T　　Yes, we've had that.

39. P　　The vegetables are grown.

40. T　　The vegetables are grown . . . Where will they be grown
　　　　do you suppose?

41. P　　At the allot . . . er.

42. P　　Erm . . . farm.

43. T　　Yes?

44. P　　Farm . . .

45. T　　Farm.

44. P [cont.]　. . . that . . . er . . . the . . . they change 'em for the
　　　　clothes, and all that. They aren't really local trade 'cos
　　　　they come from other . . . er . . . cities.

46. T　　Yes, good, that's . . . that's the next kind of trade we
　　　　are coming on to in a minute, just remember what you
　　　　said there for a moment . . . that's quite right.

Using the example of bananas, the teacher leads the class to the idea that if perishable goods are unsold this will diminish a trader's profits.

46. T [cont.] Local trade ... now these vegetables and fruit ... perhaps I'd better tell you ... these vegetables and fruit ... if you keep ... bananas ...

47, 48. Ps [several] They go bad. They go bad. [Laughter]

46. T [cont.] ... for a few days, what happens to them?

49, 50, 51. Ps [three children] They go sour. They go mouldy. They go all fusty.

52. T   Yes?

53. P   They go musty ['mushy' by another child].

54. T   Mushy, yes, what's that mean?

55, 56. Ps [two children] Soft. Sir they go black.

57. T   Black ... yes ... anything else ... ?

58. P   Over-ripe ...

59. T   Over-ripe, you can't eat them can you, when they get to that state.

60. Ps [several children] You can. I do. I have. They're lovely.

61. T   You like them black? [To a girl]

62. P   Yeh ... mmm.

63. T   What if they're all black inside?

64. P   No. Uh. [Teacher laughs] Sir, you can ...

65. T   Well, some people like them and some don't ... [Loudly] But anyway, when they get to that state, are people going to pay top price for them?

66. Ps [several] No.

67. T   They're *not*. So the trader who's selling ... the trader who's selling *these* things ... has a problem. If he doesn't sell them quickly ... what's going to happen?

68. Ps [several] Go rotten. Go bad.

69. T   And what's going to happen to that money that he makes?

70. P   He isn't going to get as much profit.

71. T   He won't get much profit ... so local trade then ... is very often the trade that buys and sells things in the district round about ... things which won't keep for very long, or which will go bad, and so the trader ... he ... you see you can't afford to send them a long way. If you send them miles and miles and miles they'll probably be bad by the time they get there. Local trade, then, is very often concerned with things that won't keep.

After this the teacher began his presentation of 'home trade' with the warning that ' "Home" doesn't mean what you think it means'.

The above is an account of the teacher's intentions and not of what was understood by thirty or so children. To get any evidence of the latter we must look at the details of what was said, and sparse evidence it is. The question I wish to pose is: Are these pupils using language to construct meanings or are they using it for other purposes? Undoubtedly both are going on, though it seems to me that the 'other purposes' predominate.

On one or two occasions during the episode pupils are using exploratory language, and it is informative to notice when this occurs. For example, when a pupil equates 'profit' with 'money', the teacher says (No. 12), 'Yes. Can you be a little more exact than that?' which leads to the careful presentation of an example. 'Well, say you sell some cigarettes for two an ... you *bought* some cigarettes for two and er ... six and you sold 'em for two and seven you'd be making a pen ... penny profit.' In a later exchange the teacher having received the reply (No. 42) 'Farm' implicitly invites expansion of this by an encouraging 'Yes', and this calls forth exploratory sentences from two pupils (Nos. 43 and 44). It seems that these pupils do not regard the exploratory use of language as appropriate unless the teacher encourages it by some signal.

During the remainder of these exchanges the pupils' contributions are different in function. It can be seen at a glance that whereas on each occasion the teacher speaks several sentences each pupil contributes no more than a word or a phrase. It is the teacher who is using language to shape meanings, not the pupils, who are given only slots to fill with single words. This is like the kind of traditional written exercise in which pupils are required to copy out a sentence from a book, supplying only single words to fill occasional gaps in the text. Such dialogues are so familiar to anyone who has ever been a pupil in a school that it is not easy to challenge their apparent inevitability. Yet it is fair to say that, in comparison with the best of our group discussions, these pupils are not being encouraged to use the learning strategies which they possess. They are active, even vociferous, participants, but their activity lies in accepting what Bruner calls 'the expository mode'. Those children who speak are for the most part competing for the teacher's approval. The teacher's eagerness to encourage lively participation while at the same time retaining control of the ideas leads at one point to irrationality. The pupils are not given the opportunity to construct for themselves the criteria upon which the teacher's concept of 'local trade' is based. Instead the criterion which they are offered is 'this end of the market' so that their lively participation in giving examples does not contribute to an understanding of what constitutes 'local trade'. This is far from Bruner's 'hypothetical mode' or from an 'as if' attitude to alternatives. These pupils are at their teacher's mercy: if they are to understand it must be through his eyes.

In a context such as this, the pupils' existing knowledge may be seen by the teacher as a threat to the sequence which he has planned. The teacher will not put it in this way: he will either fail to understand what is said to him, or regard it as irrelevant, or see it as 'one of the clever ones who has jumped ahead'. As early as No. 4 one pupil is able to say, 'Trade is where er . . . when you trade summat or you swap something.' This is ignored while the teacher persuades other pupils to reply to his previous definition of trade. When a pupil asserts (No. 28) that clothes are sold at the near end of the market this has to be brushed aside as it does not contribute to the list of perishables, though it may well be true. When another pupil later leaps ahead with 'They aren't really local trade 'cos they come from other . . . er . . . cities' (No. 45), this is skilfully stored for future reference: not every teacher would have been able to do this. Most disconcerting is the insistence by several children that they enjoyed overripe bananas. This is dealt with by a sudden change to an authoritative voice-quality and intonation: 'But anyway when they get to that state, are people going to pay top price for them?' (No. 65), which quietens the buzz of discussion.

I am not asserting that the teacher could or should have behaved differently at any of these points: I want to say that, having adopted in advance an absolute control over the content and over the sequence of presentation, he was committed to a pattern of communication which implicitly devalued his pupils' out-of-school knowledge. The teacher's implicit view of knowledge, and of his responsibility for it, carried implications for the social order in which this knowledge was to be enacted, and (in turn) for the learning behaviour open to his pupils. This was in fact quite contrary to his expressed intentions.

More generally, this episode raises interesting questions about the relationship of a teacher's knowledge to his pupils' knowledge. (I shall ignore the choice of bananas for local trade since this is a slip which cannot be taken to be representative.) One often thinks of the pupils' knowledge as an immature version of the teacher's knowledge, which is then a kind of goal to which the learner is tending. In mathematics and the physical sciences this is probably a reasonable way of looking at it, but it seems to fit less well with the arts and social studies. In this case, the teacher with his talk of trade and profit is putting a seller's view of value, whereas those who emphasize their liking for ripe bananas are presenting a consumer's view.[10] Here we have what is not so much an immature viewpoint to be superseded as one of several valid viewpoints which need eventually to be interrelated. (The teacher is mistaken when he says (No. 32) that it is more important that shoes are made elsewhere than that they are not eatable: he is expecting his pupils to accept his frame of reference uncritically.) Any attempt to impose the one viewpoint – even though it might gain status by appearing in a book labelled 'Geography' – is quite out of place therefore: these pupils *did* have a valid viewpoint to present. A more open discussion seems essential if the children are to relate these two viewpoints sufficiently to arrive at a new and more complex action knowledge.

It is not possible in discussing an example such as this to separate the teacher's control of the social order from his control over the knowledge being enacted. It is not at all unusual for a teacher who is highly committed to the 'personal development' of his pupils, and who knows them individually, nevertheless to control classroom knowledge so tightly that in order to succeed at school they must submit to his view of things. Nell Keddie surmises on the basis of her study of lessons[11] that 'the pupils

10. I owe this point to Mrs Barbara Slaughter.
11. Keddie, N. (1971), 'Classroom Knowledge', in M. F. D. Young (ed.), *Knowledge and Control*, Collier-Macmillan. This paper is very relevant here since Miss Keddie discusses with examples many of the issues touched on briefly in this chapter.

who come to be perceived by teachers as the most able . . . are those who have access to or are willing to take over the teacher's definition of the situation', and goes on to say that this amounts in part to 'an ability to move into an alternative system of thought from that of his everyday knowledge. In practical terms this means being able to work within the framework that the teacher constructs and by which the teacher is then himself constrained'. The geography lesson from which I have quoted seems to exemplify well how the teacher's framework constrains the pupils' participation. One might go on to suggest that a teacher will be more likely to be constrained in his turn whenever his own grasp of the subject-matter is relatively external, whenever he too is in a state of dependency upon textbook and 'expert'.

4. Forces Against Exploratory Talk

In analysing the geography lesson I endeavoured to show that norms of classroom control are closely linked to teachers' views about their responsibility for controlling subject-matter. The rapid sequence of questions can be seen as a device for excluding the pupils' action knowledge by making them dependent on the teacher's sense of relevance. Every secondary school teacher will have met classes of older adolescents who do not answer teachers' questions, who will not join in pseudo-discussion of the kind represented in the geography lesson. They have learnt during the years that most teachers only wish to hear the expected reply, that they do not want discussions that include divergent viewpoints and which raise different questions from theirs. When teachers complain about classes who will not talk they often present this as a moral failing in the pupils: it is more likely that the pupils have learnt from their schooling that their knowledge is irrelevant in a context determined by teachers, examinations, school syllabuses, and so on.

School subjects offer ways of making sense of the universe which are different from those of everyday life. (English may have to be excepted from this, since many teachers of English see its task as the refinement of everyday knowledge through language.)

If we trace in imagination the development of a concept such as 'pressure' from its presence in a child's non-verbal play (pushing toys or bursting balloons), through the first introduction of the word itself (perhaps in connection with bicycle tyres), through school physics lessons to its use by the adult (perhaps now a hydraulics engineer), we shall find no sudden changes but the kind of progressive elaboration that has been described by Piaget. School subjects offer ways of interpreting the world which develop out of everyday ways of understanding. Some subjects, especially the sciences, require considerable leaps of faith, submission to periods of uncertainty before the learner can confidently use the new system to interpret the world. How can learners be supported through this period of anxiety? How can teaching hurry forward the moment when the new system makes sense? I do not believe that we can hurry on the time when the learner is able to explain how a syphon works by excluding from discussion his earlier and more primitive conception of pressure. Quite the reverse, since it is this conception that needs to be modified. Nor (I believe) do we help the learner by emphasizing his ignorance and dependence on the teacher's expert knowledge. For these reasons the over-control of knowledge by teachers must in the long run hinder learning, whatever social functions it performs then and there in the classroom.

In everyday conversation we support one another's sense of reality whenever we reply. The teacher who replies to a colleague's remark about dinner money implicitly confirms the meaningfulness of weekly totals and naughty pupils who forget their money. An appropriate reply confirms that the original remark meant something. It is useful to consider teacher's replies to their pupils in this light. How far do they confirm the reality of their pupils' world? As Bellack has shown, teachers usually respond to what their pupils say not by replying to it but by evaluating it.[12] (This is true also of what teachers write at the end of their pupils' written work.) Gumperz makes an interesting surmise about the

12. Bellack, A. A. et. al. (1966), *The Language of the Classroom*, Teachers College Press. Nearly one-third of all teachers' moves were categorized as 'Rating'; this included less explicit forms of acceptance and rejection.

recorded under advantageous conditions: it is not easy in an ordinary lesson to create the sense of occasion generated when four pupils leave their lesson to be recorded by a strange and portentous gentleman from the university.

But teachers will wish to know what alternatives there are to teacher-dominated discussion. How can pupils be given a more active part in learning without being abandoned to their own devices? Connie and Harold Rosen have shown that a teacher's guidance need not be dominating, that he can have a sense of direction without pre-empting what his pupils should say. (The next chapter may indicate why it is that such teachers are not easy to find, especially in secondary schools.)

Group work *can* contribute valuably to some kinds of learning, so long as the groups are not left unsupported. It is not my main intention to offer practical advice to teachers, so I have relegated to an appendix some notes on the setting-up of group tasks, and the sequential planning of small-group and full-class discussions (see p. 191). It must be remembered, however, that many pupils are so habituated to direction from teachers that its withdrawal makes them anxious or rebellious.

A very different alternative to the traditional question and answer is exemplified by Mrs M. Pyrah of Castleford, who has shown that ten- and eleven-year-old pupils can conduct public dialogue of a quite unfamiliar kind. Mrs Pyrah taught an un-streamed class of primary school children during their last year in the school, and took charge of them for nearly the whole of their week in school. The school is set in a council estate in a small mining town; many of the children's fathers are miners. For part of each day the children sat at tables, mostly engaged in reading, writing or painting, and while they sat there they sustained a public debate. They spoke about books they had read, and recommended them to one another, or about plants and animals they had seen, or things they had done. Occasionally a child would show to the class a piece of work in progress, perhaps a painting, and ask for criticism and advice. Mrs Pyrah seemed to play little part in this: occasionally she put in a word to guide the topic or to 'correct' a low-status dialect form used by a pupil. But most of the dialogue was guided by the pupils themselves, so that it continued even if the teacher left the room. When one child finished he might ask a question to invite another by name to contribute, but there was no interruption, or competition to speak. Here is a short extract from one such discussion, enough to give the flavour:

P.1   Recently I dissected a young sparrow ... The first things I removed were its legs and wings. It hadn't any wings as I guessed it was only about two days old. The wings were very soft and rather like jelly ... When I removed the heart it was red and seemed very ... as if it was full of blood and it had some rather large blood vessels from it. Also I ... was surprised to find that the eyes were ... took up most of the head. And the brain was only very small. I found the stomach which was like a turquoise marble in its stomach ... When I took a longitudinal section out of it I found there was a green mash. This had some little ... black shiny little things in and I found these were the wing coverers ... of a beetle. Also I found some red grit which the mother had fed the babies.

Teacher   They are wings ... You said wing coverers ...

P.1   Oh, they are the actual wings ...

Teacher   I think so.

P.2   I have also done some dissections ... and few ... my last one was of a mole. First of all I cut the head the ... feet off as I always do this because it ... it gives less er resistance to ... so you can easily cut the body then. When these have been removed I cut open the head and ... trim most of the fur off and then I split the skull. Most of the brain ... inside ... remained and er just a bit of it came out and it was er white ... like the er young blackbird er I dissected. Also when I cut the body open we had to trim most of the fur off first ... as we always do. Then we ... I er ... did ... made a lucky cut er somewhere and ... a whole mass of greyish green er fell out of the side of the mole and in this was the stomach and liver and these ... and I guessed that I had ... accidentally removed the whole of the digestive system. We cut ... we then er started cutting ... upwards and ... in a small chamber of its own we we cut through I found a red lung. This seemed to be in two parts and was red with dark red blotches on it. In between the other lung and the lung I removed was the heart. This was er ... er just like a lump of muscle except it was red and it wasn't just any shape it had er .... er exact er shape so that it could fit easily into its into between the lungs.

P.3   Yesterday my grandma told me that she had seen a magpie flying about her house. I went outside to try and find it. It was on the roof and it suddenly flew down and I thought it was going to ... bump into me but it darted quickly and it landed on the ... wall. It seemed quite tame as a boy was throwing pieces of ... pa ... white paper to attract its attention. I was walking slowly up to it and then all of a sudden it flew away. I could see its beautiful white underparts.

P.4   Instead of saying 'all of a sudden' I should just say 'suddenly'.

This represents a level of control of language not usually found in classrooms even with older children. It is impressive in vocabulary, complexity and range of grammatical structures, in the ability of the children to plan a lengthy utterance, and to collaborate in governing the progress of the discussion. Mrs Pyrah seemed to have achieved this by ceasing to control the moment by moment progress of the *content* of the lesson and instead directing her considerable authority to establishing *the mode of speech*. In my terms, the speech function in these lessons was undoubtedly 'final draft', for the utterances seemed highly preplanned and explicit.

Different opinions are possible of the educational value of Mrs Pyrah's style of discussion. Some commentators have pointed enthusiastically to the children's remarkable flexibility and resource in deploying mature language forms. Others have pointed to the rigidity of the speech style and its relative unsuitability to express feeling. But this is not my point. Mrs Pyrah has shown that it is possible to establish in a classroom *a mode of speech and control entirely alien to current expectations*. The usual pattern of teacher-pupil communication *can* be changed. What Mrs Pyrah did, others can do, in secondary as well as primary schools. A team of secondary teachers (of various subjects) might agree to set up with a particular set of pupils not one but two or three contrasting styles of discussion, and allow time for pupils to become as confident in using these styles as Mrs Pyrah's pupils were. Of course, this does imply changes in what is learnt, since some emphasis would move from the content of knowledge to the processes by which pupils come to utilize it.

6. Control by Worksheet

So far I have discussed teachers' control of their pupils' participation in lessons solely in terms of the spoken interchange which is the primary means used. Similar control can be exercised in writing, however, through work-cards or worksheets. Worksheets are primarily devices used by teache, s for controlling what their pupils do. They are mainly used when various pupils in the same room are engaged in different pieces of work. For example, a teacher in a primary school may prepare (or purchase ready-made) a set of arithmetic cards. Each card contains a number of calculation tasks. A series of such cards may be graded in difficulty, or cover a number of different forms of calculation. They are usually numbered in a set order so that each pupil, without necessarily consulting the teacher, may work through them. Thus each child in a class may be working at a different stage in the sequence, according to his speed of working, which may be related to his ability or to his assiduity. Work-cards have long been in use for certain parts of the syllabus of primary schools; their use is spreading rapidly in secondary schools, probably as a way of coping with unstreamed classes.

When teachers control pupils' work by means of worksheets, this is often referred to in books as 'individual learning' or 'individualized instruction'. The name should not prevent us from understanding the sense in which the learning activities are 'individual'. Pupils work at their own pace; the fast worker can complete more calculations, fill more pages with writing, do an extra map or drawing. In no other sense is the work 'individual'; where there are options they are open to all. The only individual characteristic catered for is that of speed. The teacher in his written persona on the worksheet is less responsive to his pupils as individuals than he is in face to face interaction with them, since his choices have to be made in advance. Nor, in most of the worksheets which can be seen in use in schools, is there much freedom for the pupil to guide his own learning, though L. C. Taylor[15], in recommending resource-based packages, claimed that they moved the emphasis from teaching to learning.

Here is an example of a worksheet prepared for use in second-year history classes in an unstreamed comprehensive school. Three standard school history textbooks were used as sources of information, and pupils are directed to them at appropriate points in the worksheets. (I have omitted their titles and referred to them as A, B, and C.)

1. *The Village* [A. Page 130; B. Pages 2–4; C. Page 22]

a) Draw and label an imaginary medieval village showing forest, commons, meadow, fields, church, houses, river, mill.

b) Study the village sketched in Reference Book A on page 130 and then answer the following:

    (i) How big was a villein's holding?

    (ii) Make a guess at the population of the village and explain how you reach your answer.

    (iii) What do you notice about the positions of the hall, the mill and the villagers' homes?

2. *The People of the Village* [A. 129–132; B. 5–10, 26; C. 20–21]

Who were: Villeins, Cottars, Freeholders, Bailiff, Reeve, Steward, Tethingmen, Constable?

3. *People's Homes* [A. 229–230] [B. 5–7, 9; C. 21]

EITHER: Describe and draw a cruck framed house. List the differences between it and your home.

    OR: Make a model of a cruck house.

4. *The Work of the People* [A. 132–5; B. 34 on; C. 23–4]

    (i) How was land split up between the people?

    (ii) Write to explain the Three Field System of farming.

    [Describe the crop rotation used, strips, fallow, commons]

    (iii) EITHER: Write a short scene describing the discussion of a villein and a modern farmer about the merits and disadvantages of the Three Field System.

15. Taylor, L. C. (1972), 'Resource-based learning in British secondary schools', *British Journal of Educational Technology*, 3:2.

OR: List the advantages and disadvantages of the
Three Field System.

(iv) Draw sketches to show the various kinds of work done by a
villein during the year. OR

Make up a calendar, picturing the work to be done each month.

5. *Their Amusements* [A. 231–2; B. 55–69; C. 25 and 64]

(i) Briefly describe how you spend your Sunday.

(ii) Describe how villagers spent a Sunday in medieval days, writing
and/or drawing about all the games they might have played.

6. *Their Food* [A. 229–31; B. 18–20; C. 31–3]

(i) List menus for a day's meals today.

(ii) List menus for a day's meals in 1300 for

A) A villein
B) A lord of the manor.

7. *Law and Order* [A. 131–2; B. 69–82; C. 38–41]

Write or illustrate a scene in a medieval manor court, showing
THREE typical offences, how the offenders were caught, how a
decision about their guilt was reached and what punishments were
ordered.

This worksheet is not quoted here to be pilloried; it offers a
thoughtful and even imaginative range of tasks. It would not be
difficult in some schools to find worksheets which limited pupils
to largely mechanical copying activities.

As a form of communication, worksheets have two marked
characteristics: they isolate the learner with his task, and they
keep control firmly in the teacher's hands. Why are these twelve-
year-old pupils being asked to write and draw? What is to be
the function of their activities? Let us look more closely at this
particular example. For what audience are pupils to write in
answering Question 2? I suspect that if we look it will turn out
that what they write is very different from the kind of jottings
which we make for ourselves. Why then should they write about
villeins, cottars and so on if they are not writing for themselves?
They are certainly not giving new information to the teacher who
set the question. Probably they are writing in order to show their
teacher that they have done the task set them. This is the kind
of audience which the London University Writing Research
Unit has called 'The Teacher as examiner'. The same is prob-

ably true of Questions 4, 6, and 7, in all of which the central purpose is to require pupils to rehearse information which they have obtained from reading several pages in the three school textbooks provided.

Writing a summary for someone who knows already and whose main interest is in discovering whether you have completed some reading is not a very demanding task. It places little pressure on the pupils to make their learning explicit to themselves. Contrast what happens when we have to explain to someone who genuinely does not understand; our struggle to foresee their needs and re-shape the knowledge for them is likely to change our own grasp of that knowledge. In its very nature the worksheet widens the gap between the child who writes, and any imaginable demand on him for explicitness. Who reads worksheets? What sort of 'reply' did the history teacher usually offer to what was written: the kind of reply which we expect deeply affects the way we talk or write. The very impersonality of the worksheet must tend to turn the tasks into routines except for the minority of pupils who become imaginatively involved in the study of medieval life. (Worksheets *can* be used as devices for provoking pupils, alone or in groups, to define tasks for themselves. The comments in this section refer to worksheets as I have commonly observed them in use in secondary schools, though I have chosen an example which seems more thoughtfully planned than some I have seen. The teacher who wrote this worksheet accepts the general thesis of this section, but comments firstly that worksheets constitute only part of the work done in history lessons, and secondly that a far wider range of resources would normally be available.)

The worksheet however, because it is interposed between the teacher and the pupil will tend to minimize the likelihood that the teacher's interest in the subject matter will be communicated to his pupils. The teacher who wrote this worksheet clearly believed that imaginative insight into the lives lived by people in other times is a significant part of historical knowledge, at least for twelve-year-old pupils. This is how I interpret tasks such as No. 5. It seems all too likely that this too will be interpreted by many pupils as a test of the information they have drawn from the books. The success of these questions must depend largely on this teacher's ability to move quickly round the class while they are working, helping individuals to interpret the questions and, in a brief dialogue, showing himself to be an interested audience for whatever his pupils are to write.

Pupils working alone do not constitute the sole alternative to a teacher facing a class and controlling whatever they say. Both the traditional teacher-dominated lesson and the mode of working implied by worksheets are based upon an implicit distrust of children's ability to learn. Lawton and his colleagues place the practical emphasis rightly in a Schools Council pamphlet:

The teacher's task is to plan the situation so that pupils are encouraged to keep on asking the most important questions. This is much more difficult than just making available work-cards and reference books.[16]

Children *can* ask questions and formulate hypotheses: this is an ability that school should develop, not impede. (As Nell Keddie wryly points out, 'In the classroom it often seems that pupils are more enquiry-minded than teachers'.)

Bruner was right that the 'intrinsic motivation' which arises when we become personally interested in a topic is an immensely more powerful spur to learning than any 'extrinsic' rewards or sanctions which the teacher can provide. But this is not an argument for isolating pupils. Can *all* children work alone? Where does our 'interest' come from if we are not infected by the enthusiasm of others? Are there no advantages in learning side by side with other students, so that we can talk things over with them? Is it possible to encourage such talking over, and to make it as effective as possible? When do we most modify our attitudes and values, when alone or when interacting with other people?

It is easier to ask such questions than to provide persuasive answers. What appears to have created worksheets were ideas about self-guided learning which have been re-interpreted by teachers with quite different preconceptions about the nature of knowledge and about the part played by language in learning. We turn to these preconceptions in the next chapter.

16. Lawton, D., Campbell, J., and Burkitt, V. (1971), *Social Studies 8–13*, Schools Council Working Paper No. 39, Evans/Methuen Educational.

Chapter Five
Transmission and Interpretation

1. Teachers' Attitudes to Written Work

It would be a mistake to think that what a teacher teaches is quite separate from how he teaches. Books on curriculum planning often show the selection and ordering of subject-matter as a separate stage from the planning of learning activities or teaching methods.[1] It is possible to show that the way in which teachers think about what constitutes knowledge is often linked to what they think learning and teaching are. That is, a view of knowledge is likely to carry with it a view of classroom communication and of the roles of teacher and pupil in formulating knowledge.

The study which I am about to describe[2] was carried out as an inquiry into secondary school teachers' attitudes to written work. A direct approach to spoken communication would be less profitable, since we are all less aware of spoken language than of written, partly because our educational tradition has put greater weight upon writing than upon speech. Teachers of third-year classes in eleven secondary schools were asked to write down (1) why they set written work, (2) what they kept in mind when they set it, (3) what they did in 'marking' pupils' writings, and (4) what uses, if any, they made of it after marking. Their answers to these questions were categorized, and factor analysis was used to find out patterns amongst them.

Some teachers tended to give replies which fell into one group of categories; other teachers' replies avoided these categories but

1. Some writers treat 'instruction' as entirely separate from 'curriculum'. See, for example, Beauchamp, G. A. (1968), *Curriculum Theory*, The Kagg Press.
2. Barnes, D., and Shemilt, D. (1974), 'Transmission and Interpretation', in *Educational Review* 26:3, June 1974.

fell consistently into another group of categories. Thus it was possible to see the replies as falling somewhere upon a dimension which runs from a *Transmission* view of teaching and learning to an *Interpretation* view. Here are lists of those categories which fell nearer the Transmission or the Interpretation ends of the dimension.

TRANSMISSION		INTERPRETATION
Recording Acquisition of Information	(purpose)	Cognitive Development Personal Development
Product Task	(awareness)	Context Pupil's Attitude
Assessment No Follow-Up Corrections	(responses)	Replies and Comments Future Teaching Publish

From these lists of categories it is possible to build up pictures of those teachers whose answers fell into the Transmission categories and of those whose answers fell into Interpretation categories. (There were some teachers whose answers did not fall clearly into either pattern: it was not possible to tell whether this was because their views of teaching were diffuse and unformed, or whether they were systematically organized on different principles.)

A teacher whose answers fell mainly or entirely in Transmission categories saw the purpose of writing primarily as the *acquisition* or *recording* of information. When he set written work, he thought mainly of the *product* – the kind of writing which he hoped his pupils would do – and of whether the *task* he set was appropriate and clear to the pupils. He saw marking primarily in terms of *assessment*, and either handed back written work to pupils with *no follow up* or used it as a basis for the *correction* of errors.

A teacher whose answers fell mainly or entirely in Interpretation categories saw the purpose of writing either in terms of *cognitive development* or more generally as aiding the writer's *personal development*. When he set written work, he was concerned with *pupils' attitudes* to the task being attempted, and was aware of aspects of the *context* in which the writing was done, such as the audience to be addressed, the range of choices available and the availability of resources. He saw marking primarily in terms of making *replies and comments*, and was concerned to *publish* his pupils' work by various means, and to use it as the basis of his *future teaching*.

In the last two paragraphs I have indicated what kinds of answers were made by Transmission and Interpretation teachers, but this does not go far to explain why they made them, or what coherence there is in each point of view. In order to do this I shall have to go beyond the evidence and offer my interpretation of it. I can do this by quoting from the paper in which these results were published.

The Interpretation teacher sees writing as a means by which the writer can take an active part in his own learning: as pupils write they can – under certain circumstances – reshape their view of the world, and extend their ability to think rationally about it. He believes that the social context in which the writing takes place will partly determine whether it performs this function. He tries to ensure that his pupils see the written work as relevant to their own purposes, and see writing as contributing to a dialogue in which he plays a crucial part. He therefore writes replies as well as comments, gives his pupils' writings the added status of wider publication,[3] and allows it to influence the direction of lessons, thus encouraging pupils to play an active part in the shaping of knowledge.

The Transmission teacher on the other hand, is primarily aware of writing as a means of measuring the pupil's performance against his own expectations and criteria. When he sets written work his attention is focused upon the kind of writing he wants, so that he is careful to ensure that his pupils understand what he wants of them. He assumes that it is his business to define the task for his pupils, and to provide them with information about their success in measuring up to his standards. He values writing as a record to which his pupils can later look back, but assumes that they will address it to a general disembodied reader rather than to themselves or to him. He believes his main responsibility in receiving pupils' writing to be the awarding of a grade. Usually he continues with the lessons which he has already planned, and does not refer back to pupils' previous work, which he regards as completed when he hands back his assessment to pupils. On the occasions when he does mention pupils' work in class he uses

3. See the discussion on pp. 88–96 of the effect of audience upon the ways in which knowledge is shaped by talking or writing.

it either as a means of correcting errors in content or manner, or as an opportunity to emphasise to the class the need to preserve high standards in written work. On the whole he regards writing as a record for future reference rather than as a means of learning; when he does think of writing as contributing to the learning of his subject it tends to be in terms of the memorising of factual information.

Underlying these two views of written work are two contrasting views of the part played by learner and teacher in classroom communication. The Transmission teacher sees it as his task to transmit knowledge and to test whether the pupils have received it. To put it crudely, he sees language as a tube down which knowledge can be sent; if a pupil catches the knowledge he can send it back up the tube. Such a teacher does not see speech or writing as changing the way in which the knowledge is held. For the Interpretation teacher, however, the pupil's ability to re-interpret knowledge for himself is crucial to learning, and he sees this as depending on a productive dialogue between the pupil and himself. This is why he emphasizes the context for writing, and the importance of making responses of various kinds to what is said or written, since these will support the learner's attempts to interpret. A Transmission teacher thus gives to his pupils a much more passive role in learning than does an Interpretation teacher.

2. Communication and Specialist Subjects

When we looked at the teachers' replies to these questions in terms of the subjects which they taught we found a substantial relationship between the subject and the teacher's position on the Transmission-Interpretation dimension. The teachers of biology and physics formed coherent groups on the Transmission side of the dimension. Teachers of chemistry, languages, and domestic science also tended to the Transmission side but they were more dispersed and on average less extreme in their views. Teachers of history and geography were even less predictable, varying almost equally towards the Transmission and Interpretation poles. Teachers of religious education and English were both widely dispersed but mainly on the Interpretation side, with English teachers taking on average, a considerably more extreme position. However, it would be a mistake to take these tendencies too seriously, for the numbers for each subject were not large. Although most science teachers held Transmission views it would not be difficult to find some with Interpretation views; although most English teachers held Interpretation views it would not be difficult to find some with Transmission views.

It seemed from our analysis that a teacher's position on the scale was about equally determined by his subject and by other factors. It was as if a teacher when he is trained to teach history, or science, or English, learns not only his subject matter but also a view of what constitutes teaching and learning in that subject. But this alone does not determine his view of classroom communication. One can only guess at those aspects of a teacher's personal history which also have influence: I suspect that teachers' views of what should go on in lessons are often related to deep-seated personality traits.

What is there about these school subjects that makes specialist teachers arrange themselves in this order?

> Science
> Languages
> Domestic Science
> Geography and History
> Religious Education
> English

It should be noted that teachers of science and of languages were not only nearest to the Transmission end of the scale but also were more homogeneous in their views than were teachers of any other subject. In effect, specialism in a science or in a language seemed to place stronger constraints upon teachers than did specialism in other subjects. (The widest scatter was in geography, which reminds one that this is an arts subject in some universities and a science subject in others.)

In both science and languages most teachers perceive themselves to have access to coherent and public bodies of knowledge which their pupils' everyday experience does not give them access to. Most English teachers do not believe themselves to hold a unique body of knowledge which is out of their pupils' reach, but see themselves as helping pupils to extend and refine the knowledge and skills which they use in everyday life. Teachers of history, geography and especially religious education are in a more ambiguous and intermediate position. The characteristics of all these subjects are not eternally immutable but the result of their historical development. Two generations ago English teachers for example laid far greater emphasis than at present upon access to an authoritative literature and to preferred styles of literacy. Teachers of religious education, although presumably having access to a unique body of knowledge, today often prefer not to emphasize this view of their subject, but seek rather to extend and refine their pupils' existing moral understanding and discriminations. In these two school subjects at least one can trace within recent years redefinitions of the nature of their knowledge which moves them closer to 'Interpretation'.

Thus I am hypothesizing a relationship between (1) the teacher's view of knowledge, (2) what he values in the pupils, (3) his view of his own role, and (4) his evaluation of his pupils' participation. Here are these four laid out formally:

The Transmission teacher . . .	*The Interpretation teacher . . .*
(1) Believes knowledge to exist in the form of public disciplines which include content and criteria of performance	(1) Believes knowledge to exist in the knower's ability to organize thought and action
(2) Values the learners' performances insofar as they conform to the criteria of the discipline	(2) Values the learner's commitment to interpreting reality, so that criteria arise as much from the learner as from the teacher
(3) Perceives the teacher's task to be the evaluation and correction of the learner's performance, according to criteria of which he is the guardian	(3) Perceives the teacher's task to be the setting up of a dialogue in which the learner can reshape his knowledge through interaction with others

(4) Perceives the learner as an uninformed acolyte for whom access to knowledge will be difficult since he must qualify himself through tests of appropriate performance

(4) Perceives the learner as already possessing systematic and relevant knowledge, and the means of reshaping that knowledge

---

At least half of the teachers who replied to the questionnaire saw writing as part of a transmission-assessment process which gave the learner little or no opportunity to relate the new knowledge to old.[4] For them, written work is primarily a performance, a display of well-organized knowledge in a form ready for assessment. Writing as a means of recording or memorizing is emphasized at the expense of writing as a means of learning. Such writing fails to co-opt the learner's existing purposes and understandings; it has no part in the real world, but is merely an exchange of writing for numerical marks. Similarly, by contenting himself with assessment rather than replying, the teacher makes unlikely a negotiation between the pupil's view of the world and the new knowledge.

The most unexpected result of the Transmission-Interpretation study has not yet been mentioned. Replies which were categorized as 'Cognitive Development' – those which presented writing as a way of persuading pupils to think for themselves, including deductive thinking and the correlation and interpretation of information – these were made mainly by Interpretation teachers. Musgrove and Taylor have written that current education theories 'have removed the emphasis in teaching from intellectual exchange to social relationship'.[5] The evidence of this study would seem to contradict this. It is precisely those teachers who value social relationships who also value intellectual exchange. What Transmission teachers value is the memorizing of established knowledge.

4. The Writing Research Unit at University of London Institute of Education has shown that in secondary schools there is a predominance of what I have called 'final draft' writing. See Britton, J. N., *et al.*, *The Development of Writing Abilities 11–18*, Macmillan (In Press).

5. Musgrove, F., and Taylor, P. H. (1969), *Society and the Teacher's Role*, Routledge & Kegan Paul.

3. Knowledge, Communication and Learning

It is now time to examine the relationship between Transmission-Interpretation and some of the other ideas which have been discussed, particularly the distinction between School Knowledge and Action Knowledge and Watson and Potter's distinction between Presentation and Collaboration.[6] (The following diagram is intended to have the status of a hypothesis; the relationships which it presents are open to investigation.)

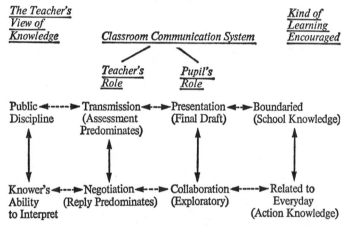

The strong vertical lines represent four dimensions of classroom communication which (I hypothesize) will vary together. The horizontal broken lines represent this relationship, and in explaining the diagram I shall read across the upper line first.

If a teacher sees knowledge as existing primarily in a public discipline he will set up classroom communication so that transmission and assessment predominate. This will compel pupils to adopt a mainly presentational performance in which speech and writing perform 'final draft' functions. This will encourage

6. See pp. 79–85 for a discussion of school and action knowledge (and also Section One of Chapter Eight) and pp. 109–13 for discussion of Watson and Potter.

boundaried learning in which the new knowledge is not brought into relationship with the learner's purposes and interests.

If a teacher sees knowledge as existing primarily in the knower's ability to interpret, he will emphasize the reply aspect of his classroom role, thus making possible a negotiation between his knowledge and his pupils' knowledge. This will open to them a collaborative approach in which the exploratory functions of speech and writing predominate. This will encourage pupils to relate new knowledge to their existing purposes and interests.

Such a model of classroom communication is highly idealized. Few teachers are likely to show purely transmission or purely interaction behaviour. More important, if pupils find that the school as a whole rejects their purposes and what they see as the real world, they are unlikely to adopt a collaborative approach in one teacher's lessons.

4. Education for Life

At this point some readers may well be retorting, 'Why not? Why should not teachers see themselves as handing over the ready-made knowledge of their specialisms? That's what they're there for.' This is a question that might be answered in two ways: that is, one might argue that restricting pupils' participation inhibits *all* kinds of learning; or one might argue that restricting pupils' participation inhibits only certain kinds of learning, and that these are the more valuable kinds. This latter reply carries with it the need to demonstrate that these kinds of learning *are* the more valuable kinds, either at this present cultural moment or from some universal viewpoint.

Now it is undoubtedly true that certain cultures have cherished bodies of arcane knowledge which were handed over to initiates in the form of rote-learning: this provides an extreme form of knowledge which the learners were not required to shape to their own use. Knowledge which is available to shape action – as opposed to knowledge which is held to be valuable in itself, perhaps because of its scarcity – needs to be reflexive and adapted by the learner to his purposes. The knowledge at present taught in our schools seems to be an amalgam of both kinds, and moreover to be currently changing. Thus it seems proper to utilize an Interpretation model of learning wherever education is seen as a 'preparation for life' rather than as initiation into a mystery.

It is useful to regard in this light the current emphases on what are called 'the humanities'. From one point of view, the humanities represent an effort to redefine history, geography and so on in a way that makes them less arcane and more easily related to the knowledge which pupils live by. School learning thus becomes not an introduction to entirely new orders of knowledge, but a sharpening, refining and reordering of knowledge which the child is already using. Clearly this accords well with the Piaget-Bruner view of learning as the successive recoding of experience. It is R. M. Jones[7] who provides the classic arguments for relating new knowledge to old. He writes, for example, of showing to children of primary school age a clip of film in which a young seagull, threatened by an older seagull, engages in submission routines to pacify the older bird. He illustrates with quotations from the lesson his assertion that the children could not understand what the seagull was doing until they had put into words their own experiences of adult aggression and the devices which they used to pacify adults. It was not just that the new knowledge could be used to make new sense of the old, but that the new had little meaning for the learner until it was brought into relationship with the old. In so far as we regard education as preparation for life, R. M. Jones's argument must carry great weight.

Recent educational literature is full of facile generalities about 'education for change' which should be treated with careful scepticism. Nevertheless, it is not unreasonable to relate the move away from arcane knowledge to a characteristic contemporary awareness of cultural change and relativity. If knowledge is regarded as 'content', the valued possession of a group, teaching becomes a package-deal. The teacher offers his own values and habits of mind wrapped up inextricably with his subject-matter; his pupils are faced with a take-it-or-leave-it. If we wish to encourage pupils to be able to adapt to new problems, and to

7. Jones, R. M. (1970), *Fantasy and Feeling in Education*, Harper & Row.

take responsibility for their own actions rather than to follow custom, then a passive view of learning will not do. In making the ethical decision to prepare pupils for choice and responsibility, teachers implicitly choose also an Interpretation view of learning. What is of practical interest is that a large proportion of teachers who would publicly assert their ends to be a world of self-responsible and flexible people do not in fact will the means which are required. That is, they see teaching primarily as an act of transmitting existing knowledge, minimizing the part actively played by pupils. This puts a premium upon routine performances. School learning becomes a special form of activity which need not impinge upon the pupil's life outside school and the values which inform it. Teaching in which Transmission predominates is the negation of 'education for living'.

The question why teachers should not transmit ready-made knowledge has now been answered: restricting pupils' participation in negotiating knowledge inhibits just those kinds of learning which many teachers today claim to be the most important. It may be that many teachers are claiming to have educational goals which are negated by what they in fact do in lessons. But to advocate an Interpretation view of education is not to argue that teachers should never present knowledge to their pupils, but rather to imply that certain patterns of communication should follow the presentation, as pupils negotiate their own ways of grasping the knowledge thus presented.

5. Classification and Framing

Basil Bernstein has put forward the theoretical constructs 'classification' and 'framing' in an attempt to clarify discussion of the form of knowledge and its relationship to the control of knowledge. 'Classification' refers to the strength of the boundaries between subjects; thus teachers of biology distinguish their subject matter sharply from mathematics, even though considerable mathematical knowledge is required in examinations in biology.[8]

8. I owe this observation to Mrs E. E. Norris.

'Framing' refers not to the form of knowledge but to the control of knowledge. Bernstein's first definition is:

This frame refers to the degree of control teacher and pupil possess over the selection, organisation and pacing of the knowledge transmitted and received in the pedagogical relationship.[9]

If one asks oneself how pupils *could* control the formulation of knowledge in the classroom, the answer must be that they would utilize knowledge brought from outside, including their everyday lives. This leads to a second definition, in which framing is related to:

... the strength of the boundary, the degree of insulation, between the everyday community knowledge of teacher and taught and educational knowledge.

Thus framing is a more complex concept in that it refers not only to the possibility of taking part in the shaping of knowledge, but also relates this to the possibility of utilizing everyday knowledge. For example, sociology can be studied so that concepts such as 'role' and 'status' are given special meanings which are intended to provide the basis for a different explanation of social processes from that available to the man in the street. Another sociologist might dispute this and see the concepts of the subject as codifications of the man-in-the-street's knowledge. One would expect the second sociologist to give his pupils opportunities to talk about their social experiences in order to reflect systematically upon them, and the first sociologist to present the concepts as stipulative definitions. It is perhaps a little surprising that Professor Bernstein has chosen to make the low boundary between school knowledge and everyday knowledge an aspect of framing rather than of classification.

Neither classification nor framing is concerned with any absolute characteristic of knowledge. Both refer to the way in which the practitioners of a subject conceive of its knowledge, and the

9. Bernstein, B. (1971), 'On the Classification and Framing of Educational Knowledge', in M. F. D. Young (ed.) (1971), *Knowledge and Control*, Collier-Macmillan. This paper came to hand while work was in progress on the Transmission-Interpretation study, and influenced the conclusions arrived at.

way in which it may be controlled. It therefore should be possible to relate to them the discussion of Transmission and Interpretation, and particularly the four aspects listed previously (pp. 144–5). Three aspects are clearly ways in which high or low framing would show itself; these are (2) those aspects of the learner's behaviour valued by the teacher, (3) the teacher's perception of his task, and (4) the teacher's perception of the learner. It is harder to place (1), the teacher's view of knowledge, since the Transmission teacher's view of knowledge as a public discipline would be a matter of high classification, whereas the Interpretation teacher's view of knowledge as the knower's ability to organize his thoughts would be a matter of low framing. This antithesis seems valid, even though it cuts across Bernstein's distinction between classification and framing. As I have noted above, the concept of framing is itself not fully separated from classification, so this should remind us that all such distinctions are explanatory tools with a status no more than hypothetical.

A Transmission teacher is likely to defend fiercely the boundaries of his subject, and be quick to dismiss non-specialists (pupils and colleagues alike) as unqualified to hold opinions about it. An Interpretation teacher is more likely to hold his knowledge in a more flexible way, and to allow that his pupils' everyday understandings have some relevance to it. A Transmission view is often associated with strong commitment to a specialist subject. The more a teacher sees knowledge as a valued possession associated with his present status and future aspirations, the less of a part one might expect him to accord to his pupils in shaping the knowledge which is given public recognition in his lessons. That is, 'the teacher as expert' is likely to have corresponding assumptions about his pupils as learners, and about the nature of knowledge and learning.

It might well be argued that there is no reason why teachers of specialist subjects might not be persuaded to change their expectations about classroom learning activities and this can easily be conceded. In the course of the Nuffield projects, groups of highly specialized science teachers have redefined not only the content of science curricula but also the learning activities required of pupils. On the other hand, it would be a valuable empirical study to estimate the proportion of teachers using Nuffield equipment and schemes of work who nevertheless maintained traditional teaching-learning procedures in their classrooms. The organization of knowledge into subjects which become quasi-institutions militates against such changes, and encourages the teacher to view himself as a subject expert and to give his attention more to the goals of knowledge than to the processes by which pupils attain them.

It is no doubt for reasons such as these that Bernstein explicitly refused to treat classification and framing as mutually dependent.

It is important to realise that the strength of classification and the strength of frames can vary independently of one another. For example, it is possible to have weak classification and exceptionally strong framing.[10]

Bernstein's example of this is the use of programmed learning to teach integrated studies. This is possible but unlikely, for when programming is used it is almost always in subjects in which teachers believe that they can exhaustively specify the objectives of learning without reference to the learners' contributions. However, the relationship which I am proposing between teachers' attitudes to knowledge and to classroom communication must neither be rigid nor unaffected by other considerations.

6. Teachers and their Knowledge

What does his knowledge mean to a teacher? It is his stock in trade, part of his claim to expertise. A secondary teacher during his specialist course at college or university will have learnt to identify himself more or less strongly both with the knowledge and skills of his subject and with the implicit styles of speech and ways of going about things which every subject depends upon.[11]

10. Bernstein, 'On the Classification and Framing of Educational Knowledge', in Young, *Knowledge and Control*.

11. J. R. Ravetz has shown in *Scientific Knowledge and its Social Problems* (Oxford, 1971) that implicit knowledge and judgement play a necessary part in all of the processes by which public scientific knowledge is constructed.

For many secondary school teachers their self-respect and hopes for promotion – indeed parts of their very identity – become bound up with their subject.

Not all teachers or all schools are alike. Even amongst secondary teachers – as Kob showed in a study carried out in Germany[12] – some see themselves primarily as teachers of a subject and others primarily as teachers of children. That is, a teacher's consciousness of his proved classroom skills, of having his colleagues' respect and of commanding his pupils' obedience, gives an alternative basis for his self-respect.

Dennis Warwick, using Waller's conflict model of teacher-pupil relationships,[13] has pointed out that the teacher's need to maintain control over pupils and desire for promotion both contribute to the maintenance of school subjects separated by a high boundary from everyday knowledge. Warwick writes:

Waller's model of the school is one that assumes the inevitability of conflict between staff and pupils because of the creation and maintenance of two divergent sub-cultures by these groups. The more that teachers are concerned for controlling dissident pupils, the more they are likely to be willing to support the strategy of parcelling out subjects into graded courses, putting emphasis on facts to be learnt and stressing the necessity of examinations at the end of each course. Concern for career mobility also leads to the support of the same strategy, because in many ways teacher quality is most easily assessed in terms of the examination results of pupils and the standards of achievement which are expected of pupils. The subdivision of subjects into teachable units makes it easier to maintain acceptably high standards at the same time as achieving a high pass rate among pupils.[14]

Warwick associates a Transmission view of teaching – including emphasis on facts and on the examining, grading and testing of pupils – with the teacher's need to maintain control of his pupils. All of these enable teachers to reward those kinds of knowledge

12. Kob, J. (1958), 'Definition of the Teacher's Role', in A. Halsey, J. Floud, and C. A. Anderson, (eds.) (1961), *Education, Economy and Society*, Free Press.

13. Waller, W. (1932), *The Sociology of Teaching*, Wiley.

14. Warwick, D. (1974), 'Some Aspects of the Sociology of the Curriculum', in M. Flude and J. Ahier (eds.), *Educability, Schools and Ideology*, Croom Helm.

which they approve of, and thereby to sponsor for further education those pupils who conform to their wishes. If an Interpretation view of learning is put into effect the teacher will have less formal control over his pupils, and will therefore have to resort to persuasion and argument, thus making his own position more uncertain. Warwick also suggests that a Transmission policy makes it easier for the teacher to demonstrate his competence to his superiors when he is looking for promotion.

One would expect teachers in primary schools to place less emphasis on subject matter and more on their relationship with pupils, since most are not likely to have identified themselves with expertise in one subject. When a modified form of the Transmission-Interpretation questionnaire was given to some primary teachers, their replies, though spread over a wide range, tended more to the Interpretation end of the scale than did those of secondary teachers. There seemed to be no clear relationship between the main subjects which teachers had studied in college and their position on the Transmission-Interpretation scale. The only clear patterning found (in a rather small sample) was that teachers with only a few years' service – who were usually teaching younger pupils – tended not to have taken up a clear position, whereas more experienced teachers expressed views clearly identifiable as Transmission or Interpretation.[15]

Primary teachers are much more 'visible' then secondary teachers (who can shelter behind their department and the subject mystique) and are therefore more open to influence by headteacher and visiting adviser, who usually control their prospects of promotion. Teachers in middle schools and in interdisciplinary teams in some secondary schools may be similarly placed. It will be considerations such as these which will decrease the influence of the subject upon teachers' views of appropriate classroom communication.

15. I am grateful to Mary Finn and Jean Froggett for permission to refer to this unpublished study.

7. Pupils and their Knowledge

If secondary school teachers are very aware of their membership
of groups of specialists stretching beyond the school to colleges,
universities and professional associations, what implication has
this for their pupils? Teachers and pupils are bound together in
reciprocal communication, so that the role adopted by the teacher
as transmitter or negotiator of knowledge necessarily implies
corresponding roles for his pupils. Professor Bernstein discusses
this in terms both of classification and framing.

Strong classification ... creates a strong sense of membership in a
particular class and so a specific identity. Strong frames reduce the
power of the pupil over what, when, and how he receives knowledge
and increases the teacher's power in the pedagogical relationship.[16]

Later in the same paper he adds:

The stronger the classification and framing, the more the educational
relationship tends to be hierarchical and ritualized and the pupil seen
as ignorant, with little status and few rights.[17]

We seldom ask questions about where knowledge comes from,
why it is constituted in the form it is, who controls it and to what
ends, why a particular body of knowledge is taught to children,
or why it is taught to some children and not to others. To ask
questions such as these is to recognize that all knowledge is
constructed by men: there is no knowledge which is just THE
TRUTH. Even something so obvious as a hill does not shout
out that it is a hill; to a baby it may be no more than a splodge
on the periphery of his vision. (He will have to learn to separate
it from everything else, to understand its relationship to people
and their purposes, to give it a name, and so on.) School subjects
are not self-constituting; they were built up by men in the course
of trying to make sense of some aspects of the world. Having
built up a body of knowledge such as physics, or economics or

16. Bernstein, 'On the Classification and Framing of Educational Knowledge', in Young, *Knowledge and Control*.

17. Bernstein, op. cit.

literary criticism and having persuaded other people that this knowledge is valuable, the specialists discover that it gives them power. First, it provides them with employment and a career, and secondly with control over acolytes who wish to join them. Their knowledge becomes a commodity which they can exchange for status and wealth: notice how jealously the medical profession controls access to its expertise. Examinations play an important part both in giving accredited status to a body of knowledge, and in controlling students' access to qualifications in it.

Bernstein relates the controlling of students' access to knowledge to what he calls a 'collection code', by which he means the teaching of knowledge in separate subjects in the way we are familiar with:

Any collection code involves a hierarchical organisation of knowledge, such that the ultimate mystery of the subject is revealed very late in the educational life. By the ultimate mystery of the subject, I mean its potential for creating new realities ... Only the few *experience* in their bones the notion that knowledge is permeable, that its orderings are provisional ... For the many, socialisation into knowledge is socialisation into order, the existing order, into the experience that the world's educational knowledge is impermeable...[18]

Thus highly boundaried subjects tend to be presented to young learners as absolute unquestionable truth. Only those who have gone through a long apprenticeship and have 'qualified' themselves through examinations, are presented with a view of knowledge as fluid, questionable, open to change, 'permeable' as Bernstein phrases it. This is true not only of the physical sciences but in history and sociology for example; one hears some historians passionately reject the idea that schoolchildren can 'do history' like a historian, and some sociologists scorn the idea that students at undergraduate or even post-graduate levels are yet prepared to do 'real sociology'. It is possible to see this either as a just recognition of the ignorance of pupils or as devices to enhance the public value of the knowledge; which way you see it will depend on whether you stand inside or outside the tacit beliefs which constitute an important part of subject-membership.

18. Bernstein, 'On the Classification and Framing of Educational Knowledge', in Young, *Knowledge and Control*.

All this has implications for what pupils learn, and how they learn it.

There is a tendency, which varies with the strength of specific frames, for the young to be socialised into assigned principles and routine operations and derivations. The evaluative system places an emphasis upon attaining *states* of knowledge rather than ways of knowing.[19]

That is, pupils are expected to receive knowledge as static and closed; they are not world-makers but world-receivers. Their task is to memorize received knowledge and master standard skills; they are not expected to participate in the making of knowledge, or to devise methods for themselves. Thus Bernstein's conceptual scheme helps to explain the orientations of the Transmission teachers who saw writing primarily as the storing or memorizing of information.

More generally what is being suggested is that there is a re-lationship between knowledge and patterns of communication. The American sociologist C. Wright Mills has put it in this way:

We can view language functionally as a system of social control ... Communication must set up common modes of response in order to be communication; the meaning of language is the common social behaviour evoked by it. Symbols are the 'directing pivots' of social behaviours ... Language, socially built and maintained, embodies implicit exhortations and social evaluations. By acquiring the categories of a language, we acquire the structured 'ways' of a group, and along with the language, the value-implicates of those 'ways' ... Back of a vocabulary lie sets of collective action.[20]

The sets of collective action which we have mainly been concerned with here have been those which constitute the shared purposes and understandings of communities of subject specialists.

19. Bernstein, op. cit.
20. Mills, C. Wright (1963), 'Language, Logic and Culture', in A. Cashdan and E. Grugeon (eds.), *Language in Education*, Routledge & Kegan Paul, 1972.

Chapter Six
Communication and Failure

1. Deficiency and Interaction Explanations of Failure

It is well known that children from working-class homes tend to be less successful in school than children from middle-class homes, and that the difference in their achievements increases throughout the years of schooling.[1] The processes by which this comes about are still not well understood. Any account of them must be based on a view of the nature of communication in schools, and it is with this in mind that I propose to discuss briefly some of the explanations which have been offered.

Explanations must involve one of two views of communication. The first group of explanations, which I shall call *deficiency* explanations, presents pupils as in some way inadequate to the demands made on them by schooling: a pupil may be seen as lacking in intelligence, in motivation to succeed, in appropriate cultural experience, or a suitable language code. Deficiency explanations present learners as receivers of messages and rate them as more or less efficient; they imply a Transmission view of classroom communication. Deficiency explanations are everyday currency and will be familiar to the reader.

A second group of explanations, which I shall call *interaction* explanations, assumes that educational communication involves not only the child in interpreting the teacher's messages and behaviour but also – inevitably – the teacher in interpreting the child's. Teachers give tasks to pupils and then interpret what they do in this way or that: a six-year-old who is sent to get his coat may be seen as 'naughty', even though to a visitor's eye the naughtiness may be invisible. Each pupil in the light of his own

1. See for example Douglas, J. W. B. (1964), *The Home and the School*, MacGibbon & Kee.

purposes and understandings is meanwhile interpreting what the teacher does, often in terms of an attitude to him as an individual. (One hears from older pupils: 'You're always picking on me', and 'I'm one of the thick ones'.) Interaction explanations seek to relate the relative educational failure of working-class pupils to a mutual failure in communication between teacher and pupil, and suggest that the wider the gap between the teacher's culture and the pupil's culture, the harder it is for the pupil to gain from schooling.

A blanket phrase such as 'the teacher's culture and the pupil's culture' disguises a puzzling complexity. What aspects of the beliefs, behaviour, knowledge, and values of the children are most likely to conflict with those of a teacher *as he displays them in the classroom*? Teachers notice pupils' clothes, their cleanliness, their conformity to expected patterns of behaviour, their willingness to accept school demands. Speech probably plays a central part: teachers quickly notice readiness of speech, conformity to approved standard dialect forms ('speaking good English'), quality of voice production, use of formulae (such as 'Please can I speak to you?') in discourse with adults. This has been discussed very valuably by Frender and Lambert.[2] They begin by referring to the 'Headstart' programmes which were given to young working-class children living in the centre of a number of American cities in order to prepare them for going to school. Although full-year Headstart courses produced measurable cognitive gains these rapidly disappeared when the children began to attend ordinary schools. This is taken to support the opinion that school failure is not simply a matter of inadequacy in the children's abilities but is related to some aspect of the interaction between them and their teachers. Frender and Lambert write:

The expectations that a teacher develops about a child's ability, potential, personality and social class background will influence how she deals with him, and this will have an effect upon his scholastic achievements. One of the more prominent mediators of these expectations of

2. Frender, R., and Lambert, W. E. (1973), 'Speech Style and Scholastic Success', in R. W. Shuy (ed.), *Sociolinguistics: Current Trends and Prospects*, Twenty-Third Annual Round Table on Languages and Linguistics, Georgetown University Press.

the child's potentials and personality may be his style of using language...[3]

The research done by Lambert and his associates goes some way to support their view that speech plays a central part in teachers' expectations of pupils, though the report scrupulously emphasizes that these explanations must be taken as tentative.

Bernstein's theory of sociolinguistic codes can now be considered in terms of the two kinds of explanation. The theory has so often been ⸱·tten about that it seems unnecessary to describe it in detail here, so I shall assume that the reader already has some acquaintance with it.[4] The theory sets out to identify one aspect of speech which is said to differentiate lower working-class from middle-class families and to account for differences in their educational achievement. It is suggested that whereas everyone at times uses language in relatively inexplicit ways which depend upon tacit knowledge shared by speaker and hearer (Restricted Codes), those people who have been brought up in middle-class homes switch more readily to using language to make explicit their underlying assumptions and beliefs (Elaborate Codes). The theory goes on to suggest that using language in this latter way makes for reflexive thought, insight into underlying principles, and the ability to see one's own point of view as open to change.

The theory has been frequently vulgarized: it can all too easily be used by middle-class people to feed their prejudices about working-class ways of life and a comfortable sense of superiority. Recently its author has gone to some pains to say that he is not presenting middle-class culture as intrinsically superior, and that he is not saying that working-class people cannot switch to elaborated codes under some circumstances. It is important to remember that the theory is still a set of hypotheses, and therefore open to challenge, modification or dismissal.

One common misconception is to transmute the idea of an 'elaborated code' into a disembodied language skill, a special

3. Frender and Lambert, 'Speech Style and Scholastic Success', in Shuy (ed.), *Sociolinguistics: Current Trends and Prospects*.

4. Readers who are not conversant with the theory are recommended to consult A. Cashdan and E. Grugeon (eds.) (1972), *Language in Education: A Source Book*, Routledge & Kegan Paul, sections III and VI.

verbal ability (like I Q, perhaps) which some pupils 'have more of' than others. This is certainly not Bernstein's intention. Unfortunately this reading of the theory fits comfortably into traditional staff-room ways of talking about children's language, and generates self-confirming beliefs. A teacher can tell that working-class pupils' language is 'Restricted Code' because he can recognize working-class children by their speech: the argument is perfectly circular. The speech characteristics seen as Restricted may however be the use of low-status dialect forms and intonations, which are very different indeed from the differences in the social functions of language which Bernstein set out to identify. Thus one now hears teachers use the phrase 'Restricted Code' to sum up their negative assessment of certain pupils' speech and writing, so that it reinforces the tendency to perceive these pupils as ineducable, and their viewpoints as invalid. Which pupils these are is of course another matter.

Thus, whatever Bernstein's intentions, his theory has frequently been taken to offer a deficiency explanation of educational failure; working-class children are thought to lack the ability to use language for the explicit organizing of thought, therefore finding it harder to respond to the cognitive demands of schooling.

Harold Rosen has pointed out[5] some of the characteristics of schools which make this unlikely to be true. As we have seen, the standard question-and-answer pattern of teaching makes little or no demand on pupils to think aloud, so that lack of the habit of verbal elaboration is unlikely to impede them in learning. Moreover (as Bernstein himself has pointed out) much school knowledge is presented to pupils as bodies of information to be learnt. When knowledge is presented as complete and not open to modification there will be little pressure towards insight into principles, so that one would expect mere reproductive abilities to be required, rather than those implied by the term 'Elaborated Codes'. Much of this knowledge depends too upon implicit assumptions of which even teachers are unaware. All this would

5. Rosen, H. (1972), *Language and Class: A Critical Look at the Theories of Basil Bernstein*, in D. Holly (ed.), *Education or Domination?*, Arrow Books, 1974: a valuably forthright presentation of the case against some aspects of Bernstein's theory.

lead one to think that schools put a premium on certain kinds of Restricted Codes, in that there are implicit rules and beliefs underlying what teachers say to their pupils, and that these are often not made explicit to any but a minority of older pupils, perhaps at sixth-form level. These Restricted Codes would have to be taken on trust by pupils.

The teacher is in control, and his reading of classroom events stands; he can insist on the validity of his own viewpoint and treat his pupils' insights as irrelevant. If he does treat his own implicit knowledge as self-evident and fails to respond to the messages from his pupils, he will perceive them as ignorant and unintelligent, and moreover communicate this perception to them. In writing this, I have returned to an *interaction* explanation, since I am using the idea of a cultural divide between the teacher's implicit knowledge and that of his pupils, which some cross more readily than others. A gap between teacher's knowledge and pupil's knowledge is of course implicit in the concept of 'teaching', but teachers often make it harder for some pupils than others to utilize the school's knowledge. Bernstein, discussing communication between teachers and working-class children, writes:

If the culture of the teacher is to become part of the consciousness of the child, then the culture of the child must first be in the consciousness of the teacher.[6]

Once one adopts an *interaction* view of education, it becomes as valid to see educational failure as the school's failure to understand a child's messages, as to see it as the child's failure to understand the school's messages. Here Bernstein is identifying himself with an *interaction* explanation. Indeed, the whole of the paper from which this sentence is quoted is devoted to the rejection of *deficiency* explanations.

6. Bernstein, B., 'Education Cannot Compensate for Society', *New Society*, 26 February 1970, pp. 344–7.

2. Teachers' Perceptions of their Pupils

This leads us to ask how it is that communication between some pupils and their teachers can break down almost completely by the time they reach upper secondary school. Teachers may perceive their pupils as hardworking or lazy, mature or immature, well or poorly behaved.[7] They may see them as intelligent or stupid, as co-operative or rebellious. They tend to see these as independent characteristics of pupils, as if the children were quite unaffected by classroom events or by the teacher's own behaviour.[8] This implicit characterization of a pupil is then used as a basis for interpreting his future behaviour, and for justifying the teacher's treatment of him.

Nell Keddie[9] has well illustrated how the streaming of pupils directs teachers' characterizations of them; this in turn influences what curriculum is presented to pupils in different streams. She quotes from a team of teachers who are planning the next part of a social studies course, and then summarizes:

What seems to emerge overall from the way teachers discuss teaching material in relation to pupils' abilities is an assumption that C pupils cannot master subjects: both 'the abstractions of sociology' and the 'economic implications' are inaccessible to them.

Thus the curriculum which is offered to C-stream pupils is different from that offered to A-stream pupils even when they are following the same syllabus. Moreover, they are expected to behave differently.

It is already clear that teachers are most concerned with what they perceive as the negative characteristics of C pupils' behaviour and that this is to some extent linked with expectations of appropriate behaviour that have a social class bias and differentiation. C stream pupils are

7. Nash, R. (1973), *Classrooms Observed: The Teacher's Perceptions and the Pupil's Performance*, Routledge & Kegan Paul.
8. I owe this point to Martin Hammersley of the University of Manchester.
9. Keddie, 'Classroom Knowledge', in Young (ed.), *Knowledge and Control*.

often seen to lack those qualities which are deemed by teachers desirable in themselves and appropriate to school, whereas A stream pupils appear to possess these qualities.

These expectations extend to the curriculum, so that C-stream pupils' contributions to lessons are not expected to be so relevant and valid. Miss Keddie quotes from a lesson a short discussion in which the teacher, presenting to a C-stream class the idea of the *nuclear* family, treats a pupil's contributions as invalid since they relate to the *extended* family. (The mutual incomprehension shown by teacher and pupil in this exchange is not unlike that shown in the discussion of 'local trade' which I quoted in Chapter Four.) Nell Keddie offers this as part of her explanation:

The scepticism of many C pupils, which leads them to question the teachers' mode of organising their material, means that they do not learn what may be taken for granted in a subject, which is part of the process of learning what questions may be asked within a particular subject perspective.

In this article Miss Keddie suggests an *interaction* explanation of social class differences in educational achievement. On the one hand, teachers have excessively low expectations of working-class children's ability to understand; on the other, working-class children are less ready than others to accept on trust the teacher's requirements and goals. (This is equally true of teachers who have come from working-class homes and have been socialized into versions of middle-class culture, a socialization which is powerfully continued by other teachers during staffroom chat.)

Miss Keddie's analysis deals with differences in teachers' treatment of A-stream and C-stream pupils. Major differences may equally exist within one school class, so that schooling may provide quite different experiences for two children who sit side by side in the classroom.

Nash[10] provides field descriptions which usefully illustrate how teachers consistently accept behaviour from some children which would earn punishment for others. One child may find that he is expected to be ill-behaved and stupid, and experience frequent

10. Nash, *Classrooms Observed: The Teacher's Perceptions and the Pupil's Performance.*

reprimands; he may be told that his speech is incorrect, and find that what he has to say is misunderstood or ignored. Another may find that the teacher listens to him and credits him with good sense, attributes good intentions to him, and responds appropriately to what he says. If such differences exist in the treatment of pupils then one would expect it over years of schooling to generate in pupils quite different attitudes to school learning and to the part which each can play in it. This would provide some explanation of how it happens that social class differences *increase* during the years of schooling. We must however regard the explanation as tentative: the evidence from studies by Lambert, Nash and others is not yet conclusive.

3. Children's Language Abilities

What perceptions do teachers have of their pupils' language? Some still talk about 'good English', as if one kind suited all occasions. Others commend their pupils with: 'That's a good word'. We have already noticed the subject specialist with his emphasis on 'using the correct words'. The language of children from lower working-class homes is discussed in terms of inadequate vocabulary. The so-called 'bad grammar' of a low-status dialect is somehow felt to provide an intellectually inferior instrument of thought, as if 'I aren't' carried less meaning than 'I'm not'. All these attitudes have in common that they treat language forms as important, rather than the ways in which they are used. This is, language is treated as if it were a possession earning social approval or disapproval, rather than a means by which children make sense out of what happens to them.

When in Chapter Two I discussed the exploratory language used by the groups I was certainly not concerned with 'speaking nicely' or even with 'good English'. Whatever it is that these two phrases refer to does not overlap with our concerns here. When Glyn said:

And the current . . . because there's no pressure on top of them . . . this fast-moving air don't have no pressure, it was clear that 'don't have no' is as effective an expression of thought as 'has no' would have been. There is no reason to think that the *forms* of language used in one social class dialect are any more logical, or useful for thinking, than those used in any other dialect, including the one called Standard English. If there are differences in the effectiveness of the language uses of different social groups, they do not lie in differences between the forms they have available. Nor is there any reason to think that any of the children we recorded were in any sense deficient in knowledge of a grammatical system. We have no reason to think, for example, that there are any children who *would never use* the forms of language ('They would have to . . .', 'probably', etc.) which I have used in identifying the hypothetical mode. It is clear that Group IV used them *in the recording* less than any other group, but that is no evidence that they did not 'know' them. Group I used more of these forms when carrying out the history task than the physics task. Group III used more when discussing the poem than in any other tasks.

It seems important not to underrate children's language abilities. Faced with a full classroom, a topic they feel unsure about, and a teacher's question that may conceal unforeseen implications, many children seem tongue-tied and incoherent, so that we value all the more those who can produce well-shaped replies. But this does not mean that the others cannot use language productively as a means of learning.

It is John, a boy of average IQ, who produced the admirably precise: 'The slips ripple and . . . er . . . flow away, don't they?' thus at once demonstrating close observation and a high level of linguistic skill. Nor was he incapable of at least first-order subordination: 'I'd make sure there were a fence going round . . . so no animals could get in.' (Once again it is clear that the non-standard form is as adequate to carry the meaning as the standard would be.) What we are dealing with is not anything which could be called 'an inadequate knowledge of his own language'. When we notice the relatively poor performance of John and the other boys in Group IV, we are looking at *characteristics of their use of language as a means of coping with school tasks*, and there is no reason to equate this with *inadequate knowledge* of language.

Some teachers when they talk about pupils' linguistic inadequacies put their emphasis either upon their use of non-standard forms, or upon their supposed lack of knowledge of the language, (of vocabulary for example). Now the explicit intention of this book is to place the emphasis elsewhere, upon those language strategies which contribute to learning. There is indeed considerable evidence that children vary in their use of language for organizing their thoughts and feelings; but this is a different matter from differences in social-class dialects. What I discussed in Chapter Two under the heading of 'language strategies' are some of the language uses which may be important for learning. Some pupils use such strategies very frequently, some hardly at all, but most use them in some circumstances and not in others. They all 'know' the language forms – the 'probably', the 'what if . . . ?', the 'might be' – but they do not readily use them when faced with school tasks. Why is this?

We might guess then that one factor affecting each group's use of the hypothetical mode is *how they assess the situation they are in, and the possibilities for action in it.* Thus, what we are considering is not the linguistic forms available to children, because as far as we know there aie no very significant differences between them in this, but *how they use the forms that they do have.* And this is partly a matter of how they see themselves and the situation they find themselves in, and particularly the task they have been given.[11] That is, their learning activities are not determined by their knowledge of language, nor merely by intelligence, but also by their interpretations of what is going on in the classroom and whether they can usefully take part in it. Now, as this latter is within the teacher's control this is a more hopeful thought, for the classroom setting, the learning tasks and the teacher's own classroom role can be modified.

Many teachers insist that their pupils must speak the Standard English dialect in an accent and vocal quality which approximates to local middle-class speech styles. They call this 'good English' and dismiss low-status styles as 'slovenly speech'. They do this

11. See the excellent discussion of this in Cazden, C. B., 'The Neglected Situation in Child Language Research and Education', in F. Williams (1970), *Language and Poverty*, Markham.

either in order to teach their pupils to 'speak correctly' or (with more sophistication) in order to help them to 'get a good job'. One teacher justified this by saying that if she accepted anything less than 'good English' from her pupils she would be patronizing them: 'You wouldn't let your own children talk like that, would you?' In one sense such teachers have their pupils' interests at heart. It is difficult to imagine, however, the effect on children of years of correction and inhibition of their home speech; banishing their everyday speech may for some be also banishing their everyday knowledge from the classroom. Mrs Pyrah changed her pupils' speech at the cost of imposing a rather inflexible public mode, but she saw to it that all pupils took part in discussions. Few teachers are as successful as Mrs Pyrah in this, for in general young people take their styles of speech from the group they belong to, or aspire to belong to, so that teachers may correct their pupils for years and do nothing more than inhibit their speech. I believe that the imposition of an alien style of speech is contrary to most pupils' interests, since it constitutes yet another way of excluding them from the formulation of knowledge. If pupils are to be prepared for a world in which white-collar jobs go with white-collar behaviour, what they need is an understanding of our stratified society and of the part played by speech styles in sustaining the strata: to tell them that their speech forms are 'bad English' is to tell them lies which disguise the true state of affairs.[12]

The American sociolinguist William Labov, attacking the idea

12. Consider for example the implications of this imaginary episode which is put forward as a model to American teachers of drama:

'... Jim scowls and doubles up his fists, becoming Donny. "Geez ... if I could git my hands on de guy that done it ..."

"Fine!" says the leader. "That's just the way Donny would say it, with one exception. Anybody want to take a guess about that exception?"

A hand goes up ... "Sure, I know! Jim said 'done' and 'git' instead of 'did' and 'get'. I don't think Donny would use bad English even if he were angry, do you?"

"No, I don't think so," replies the leader, obviously pleased ...' (Burger, I. B., *Creative Play Acting*, Ronald Press Co.)

The effect (and perhaps the intention) is to exclude parts of the children's everyday linguistic reality from drama lessons, and to indicate that they are to behave as if it does not exist.

that working-class children in some sense lack full knowledge of language, wrote:

The myth of verbal deprivation is particularly dangerous, because it diverts attention from real defects of our educational system to imaginary defects of the child.[13]

It is all too possible that some of the linguistic inadequacies which teachers perceive in their pupils arise from a long cycle of misunderstanding and rejection in which the school has failed to meet the pupil's needs as often as the pupil has failed to meet the school's demands. What is required is a qualitative change in teachers' awareness of language, a shift from content to process, from awareness of forms to awareness of strategies. If teachers observe how their pupils use the forms they do know, they are likely first to discover that their learning skills are greater than they seemed, and further to understand better how to help them to extend these. Insistence upon socially approved forms is all too likely to exclude many pupils from taking an active part in learning.

4. Deficiency Explanations are Unsatisfactory

Most teachers take it to be their duty to 'correct bad English' and in speech this may include the inhibition of low-status dialect forms, and of those intonations and speech qualities which go with informal and intimate relationships ('slovenly speech'), and even the excision of 'to get' and 'nice' from the vocabulary. Some of these inhibitions fall equally on all pupils, but others would penalize working-class children, and might seem to signal to them that their home speech, on which their own identity depends, has no validity in school. I know of no direct studies of this, but one might expect the effect of this upon a child's participation in lessons to be considerable. During the early years of primary schooling teachers are said to place more emphasis

13. Labov, W. (1970), 'The Logic of Nonstandard English', in Cashdan and Grugeon (1972), *Language in Education.*

upon social conformity than upon other forms of learning,[14] so that children would experience rejection of their home speech at an age when they would be unequipped to see it for what it is. School for some children may be from the very beginning an experience of rejection which affects them in a way which is quite irrespective of their capacity for taking part in school learning.

It is becoming increasingly clear that *deficiency* explanations of social class differences in education are unsatisfactory. It is not enough to see working-class homes as 'deprived', 'uncultured', characterized by emotional or social instability, for this looks all too like an outsider's comfortable view of the immense diversity of life within any such groups. Nash puts it clearly:

It is no use saying that children from low social class backgrounds do poorly at school because they are from poor backgrounds until it is known that teachers behave to them in the same way that they behave to children from higher social backgrounds. This is an assumption that is always made and never tested. It is an assumption which there is less and less reason to accept.[15]

But the communication is not only one way. Undoubtedly the pupil's willingness to join in the teacher's game for long enough to grasp the unspoken rules is a crucial part of school success, and one would expect children to differ one from another in this, and not only along the lines of social class.

We must therefore reject *deficiency* explanations of educational failure as unhelpful to any teacher who wishes to understand what happens in his lessons. The underlying assumption of deficiency explanations is that we can treat as absolute the teacher's view of what constitutes valid knowledge and appropriate learning behaviour. Although the teacher may speak for publicly instituted knowledge, he is also a person with views, preferences and prejudices of his own. So are his pupils, even the youngest ones. If teachers are to understand how some pupils become successes

14. See Jackson, P. W. (1968), *Life in Classrooms*, Holt Rinehart & Winston, and Dreeben, R. (1967), 'The Contribution of Schooling to the Learning of Norms', *Harvard Educational Review* 37:2.

15. Nash, *Classroom Observed: The Teacher's Perceptions and the Pupil's Performance*.

and others opt out, they must see how both social relationships and knowledge itself are negotiated in the course of classroom communication.

Chapter Seven
The Teacher's Responsibilities

1. Patterns in Classroom Teaching

It is a recipe for unpopularity to suggest to teachers that there are patterns in their classroom behaviour which can be described and compared with that of other teachers or with their own on another occasion. Many teachers – perhaps most – find this view of their work unpleasant or even threatening. They believe that their teaching is a unique response to what their pupils say and do, arising moment by moment during lessons. (By now it will be clear to the reader that I believe that this should be true of a substantial part of a teacher's work.) Teachers have often said to me: 'You can't really talk about teaching; it's too personal.' This aspect of teachers' feeling for their work is an important one for any attempt to understand or influence classroom communication: most teachers do not perceive themselves as dominating, as unresponsive to their pupils' viewpoints, or as carrying out ritual patterns of communication. Many say that a personal relationship between teacher and taught is a necessary basis for successful teaching. 'Personal relationship' here perhaps means that they have a warm sense of responsibility towards their pupils; Jackson[1] has shown that elementary (primary) school teachers gain much of their satisfaction in the work from watching the children grasp new ideas and skills under their guidance.

There is, however, much evidence to show that there are common patterns in teaching behaviour, and that some of these can be generalized across different levels of education and even from country to country, if we confine ourselves to highly industrialized nations. Almost all teachers appear to use the question-and-answer routine (called the 'recitation' in the United States) as a

1. Jackson (1968), *Life in Classrooms.*

way of controlling pupils' attention. I found this true in my own small study of secondary school lessons. In the United States James Hoetker[2] showed that in a sample of English lessons in junior high schools the teachers asked questions at an average rate of one every 11.8 seconds, and more rapidly still when lessons with less able pupils were taken alone. David Scarbrough showed that in lessons in London primary schools the pupils' replies became shorter as the teacher's questions became longer.[3] When this happens it is the teacher who is structuring meaning and leaving only slot-filling to the pupils. Bellack and his colleagues[4] showed how infrequently even older students (fifteen- and seventeen-year-olds) initiated a line of thought by raising a new issue or aspect of the subject. In my study of lessons with British eleven-year-olds I found only nine pupil-initiated sequences in twelve lessons. N. E. Flanders[5] on the basis of his many analyses of classroom interaction has put forward his 'two thirds' rule: two thirds of every lesson is made up of talk, and two thirds of the talk comes from the teacher (which seems a modest estimate[6]). If we accept the two thirds rule, during a forty-five minute lesson each pupil in a class of thirty will have an average twenty seconds of talk at his disposal.

Some of the researchers criticize sharply what they have observed. Marie Hughes, reporting her study of American teaching behaviour, wrote that 'the differences found amongst teachers were contributed by relatively few individuals'.[7] She found that

2. Scarbrough quotes this remarkable question: 'What is it when the tug's doing its job that enables a big ship to move quite easily when the tug isn't pulling it?' The expected answer proved to be 'Water'.

3. Scarbrough, D. (1968), 'The Language of the Primary Teacher', *English for Immigrants* 2:1.

4. Bellack A. A. *et al.* (1966), *The Language of the Classroom*, Teachers College Press.

5. Flanders, N. E. (1963), 'Intent, Action and Feedback: A Preparation for Teaching', in E. J. Amidon, and J. B. Hough (eds.) (1967), *Interaction Analysis: Theory Research and Application*, Holt Rinehart & Winston.

6. Bellack *et al.* found that in their sample of lessons in social studies taught to seventeen-year-olds, teacher speech as a proportion of all speech varied from 60 per cent to 93 per cent, with the median at 73 per cent.

7. Hughes, M. M. (1963), 'The Utah Study of the Assessment of Teaching', in A. A. Bellack (ed.), *Theory and Research in Teaching*, Teachers College Press.

teachers seldom encouraged pupils to elaborate the content of lessons:

> Students' [i.e. pupils'] questions, explorations, and personal experience were most frequently rebuffed or ignored. There was little attempt to build generalisations, to ask for comparisons, to look at alternatives and to look at consequences . . . The most common situation was that of a teacher asking a question that was answered by the recall of a discrete item or fact.

Hoetker and Ahlbrand, in their interesting paper 'The Persistence of the Recitation'[8], summarize many such studies of American classrooms, one as early as 1860. All show the predominance of question-and-answer methods, and all alike criticize them (as I have done) as unlikely to encourage the kinds of learning which educationists for generations have valued. There is no reason to think that patterns of classroom communication have been very different in the United Kingdom or in other European countries. Hoetker and Ahlbrand conclude by asking:

> What is there about the recitation . . . that makes it so singularly successful in the evolutionary struggle with other, more highly recommended methods? That is, what survival needs of teachers are met uniquely by the recitation?

Ian Westbury of the University of Chicago,[9] after quoting this question from Hoetker and Ahlbrand, makes an attempt to supply an answer to it. He decides that the questioning method is:

> . . . a *coping strategy* within the repertoire of possible methods available to the teacher that secures some task attention, gives some measure of control over the activity of students, facilitates coverage of content, and offers a drill and practice situation that leads to some, albeit more often than not a nominal, mastery of facts that carefully tailored tests require as the symbols of school learning.

Westbury here identifies four responsibilities which (in his eyes) teachers must undertake: (1) task attention, (2) control, (3) cover-

8. Hoetker, J., and Ahlbrand, W. P. (1969), 'The Persistence of the Recitation', *American Educational Research Journal* Vol. 6, p. 163.

9. Westbury, I. (1972), 'Conventional Classrooms, "Open" Classrooms and the Technology of Teaching', *Journal of Curriculum Studies* 5:2, November 1973.

age of content, and (4) practice for mastery. He believes that question-and-answer exchanges go far towards carrying out these responsibilities, and points out that they also make relatively limited demands on teachers' energies. He is careful not to make excessive claims for the learning thus fostered: when he says that the mastery of facts is often merely nominal, he is perhaps indicating that this kind of teaching does not help the learner to convert school knowledge into action knowledge.

Having shown that this style of teaching is 'adaptive to conditions in the setting of the conventional classroom', Westbury does not treat this as a justification but goes on to consider why half a century (or more) of adjurations to teachers to set up more open classroom communication has failed to effect change. He argues that 'proposals for change in classroom behaviours that do not address the issue of tasks and resources' are doomed to fail. Teachers must be supplied with alternative means of achieving task attention, control, coverage of content, and practice. 'Changes in teaching technologies *are* possible . . . when resources to permit that change are made available.' He illustrates what he means by 'resources' by referring to Dienes' blocks. A shift of emphasis from the teacher's teaching to the learner's learning can only take place through the aid of such resources: 'The students must be allowed to learn mathematical structures through an inductive examination and manipulation of physical and game-like embodiments of the concepts we are seeking to teach them.' Professor Westbury criticizes advocates of 'the open classroom' for seeking to deprive teachers of the support of conventional ways of controlling learning, while failing to offer them alternative ways of doing so, and this criticism is not entirely unjust.[10]

It is at this point, however, that Westbury's argument becomes inadequate, and it is perhaps not unfair to associate this with his use of the phrase 'the technology of teaching'. There is more

10. In Chapter Two and in the Appendix to this volume I have shown some of the ways in which materials and tasks may be partly structured in order to give pupils more control over learning without abandoning them to their own devices. My intention, however, (unlike Professor Westbury's) is to argue that it is not only materials and tasks but communication patterns in classroom and school which are likely to affect the success of such a policy.

than resources and technology underlying the question-and-answer method: as I showed in the last chapter, one must take into account whole ideological complexes, including beliefs about knowledge, about learning, and about people. As Elliot Eisner once wrote, 'Under the rug of technique lies an image of man'.[11] Westbury concedes too much in his phrases 'coverage of content', 'mastery of facts', and 'some measure of control'. A Transmission view of knowledge seems implicit in these terms. The predominance of question-and-answer techniques cannot be accounted for solely in terms of more or less efficient methods, as if all were agreed about what constitutes valuable knowledge. To understand why classroom communication is as it is we would finally have to go outside the classroom, beyond teachers' beliefs about knowledge and learning, to consider some of the functions performed by school knowledge in our society, especially in the selection of children for different courses, for different schools, and for different life-chances.

2. The Teacher's Dilemma

At the heart of teaching as we know it in our culture lies this dilemma: every child learns best when he is finding out about something that interests him; children are compelled by law to attend school, and are in the charge of teachers who are employees responsible for large numbers of them. There is an implicit conflict between the teacher's responsibility for control and his responsibility for learning: the one treats pupils as receivers and the other treats them as makers.

Jackson suggested that elementary (i.e. primary) teachers in the U.S.A. treat their pupils' divergencies from expected behaviour as more important than their success or failure in mastering knowledge.[12] 'It is violations of institutional expectations that really get under the teacher's skin.' Teachers frequently judge one another by their ability to 'keep order' in their classes; one

11. Eisner, E. W., 'Instructional and Expressive Educational Objectives', in Popham, W. J., *et al.* (1969), *Instructional Objectives*, Rand McNally.
12. Jackson, (1968), *Life in Classrooms*.

secondary teacher may commend another as 'a good discipli-
narian'. Young teachers learn to hold their pupils' attention by
a routine of quick-fire questions, and older teachers advise them
not to use alternative patterns of communication in which they
would not have face-to-face control. Thus the social order per-
petuates itself.

At the same time teachers accept responsibility for what their
pupils learn. They plan lessons, deciding in advance what information or line of reasoning they will present to their pupils. They
work from syllabuses and textbooks which specify what children
are to learn. The questioning routine which controls the pupils
serves at the same time to direct their attention to just that knowledge which the teacher has chosen for them, in the chosen order
and without unplanned divergencies. Written tasks, including
worksheets, similarly direct children's attention to the chosen
topic, and keep them quiet at their desks. The methods for directing children's attention to knowledge and for controlling their
behaviour here converge: controlling behaviour is controlling
knowledge. The communication patterns of classroom and corridor overlap with and shape the knowledge which is learnt there.

As we have seen, the language which the learner uses for
shaping his thoughts is very different from the language of control
and coercion. Joyce asserts that the induction of a student teacher
into his new role is carried out through an apprenticeship which
is 'designed to move the young teacher into the organizational
patterns of the existing educational system and into the roles of
functionaries in that system'.[13] He illustrates how the apprenticeship operates from four studies of the developing teaching styles
of student teachers.

All have included the following findings: student teachers reward
children verbally much less by the end of student teaching than at the
beginning (one half as much, in fact); they come to ask fewer questions
and fewer open questions proportionally (about 20 per cent less); and
they plan co-operatively with children about half as often by the time
student teaching is over as they did when it began.

13. Joyce, Bruce R., 'The Curriculum Worker of the Future', in R. M.
McClure (ed.) (1971), *The Curriculum: Retrospect and Prospect*, Seventieth
Yearbook of the National Society for the Study of Education.

This is how current definitions of classroom communication sustain themselves: the student teacher, his low status in the staffroom continually re-emphasized by means either subtle or brutal, can gain security and respect by adopting existing norms. Joyce believes that for real curriculum change (as against the mere show of innovation) new institutions should be set up where student teachers could collaborate in shaping a different social order instead of receiving apprenticeship into the existing order.

We have here the two main sources for the Transmission view of classroom communication: (1) the teacher's sense of responsibility for what is learnt, especially if he is a specialist in a particular subject; (2) the teacher's sense of what is proper behaviour for teachers and pupils, which he learnt as a pupil and as a student teacher. Both are of course open to change. Here is the dilemma. How can teachers carry out what they believe to be their responsibilities when these include both control of pupils' learning *and* encouraging pupils actively to formulate knowledge. In one direction lies control so strong that school knowledge remains alien to the learner (whether he rejects or plays along with it); in the other direction lies a withdrawal of guidance, so that the learners never need to grapple with alternative ways of thinking. The teacher has to find his way between the two.

Paulo Freire puts the ambiguity sharply in discussing what he calls 'banking education', education as the handing over to pupils of 'narrated content' which they can as it were put in the bank for later exchange for promotion and so on. Freire believes this to be a form of control which in the guise of conferring benefits inevitably dehumanizes and alienates. One of the characteristics of banking education he describes thus:

The teacher confuses the authority of knowledge with his own professional authority, which he sets in opposition to the freedom of the students.[14]

Freire puts forward in contrast to banking the idea of a problem-posing education in which it is the pupils' intentions which are at the centre. Education thus becomes part of a desire to change the world, instead of instruction in accepted beliefs about what

14. Freire, P. (1972), *Pedagogy of the Oppressed*, Penguin.

the world is. But Freire is a revolutionary, and it is hard to see how his view of education could be co-opted by a state education system.

3. The Arbitrary Control of Knowledge

Those who would defend a Transmission view of knowledge often take their stand on forms of knowledge publicly established by communities of scholars who collaborate to sustain high standards of responsibility and truth. How far this is an accurate description of universities need not concern us here. School knowledge seldom achieves this ideal. The view of the world put forward is sometimes just not true, even in terms of the children's knowledge. (Consider for example 'the friendly policeman' and the mutual distrust of police and adolescents in some city centres.) But my point here is not that there are systematic discontinuities between school knowledge and pupils' action knowledge, but rather that what pupils are required to learn is often highly arbitrary. There does seem to be good reason to seek ways of detaching the responsibility for the truthfulness and validity of what is learnt from the moment by moment control of dialogue.

Much teaching leaves the pupils dependent not on publicly established systems of knowledge (if such exist) but upon quite trivial preconceptions set up arbitrarily either on the spur of the moment, or when the teacher planned the lesson during the previous evening. This reduces the part played by the pupils to a kind of guesswork in which they try to home in upon the teacher's signals about what kind of answer is acceptable.

It is not in the least difficult to find illustrations of this, especially in subjects such as history or geography where the teacher is often constructing an informal and *ad hoc* collection of knowledge which will have no particular validity beyond that lesson. Here is a teacher talking to eleven-year-old pupils about deserts; she has just explained how sand is formed by the disintegration of rock.

T. Now as time goes on these tiny particles also fracture and break up and shatter until they get so small that they're able to be picked up by the wind and blown about. Now if you think of the seaside and it's been a windy day and you've been on the beach what can you tell me about the sand?

Since the question itself offers the pupils limited guidance about what aspects of sand might be in the teacher's mind, they must attempt to answer this from clues which have been dropped previously, either in the same lesson or an earlier one.

Dialogue	*Commentary*
P. It starts to fly about.	
T. Mm and something else about it when it starts flying around.	The teacher indicates that the pupil has not guessed the precise aspect of sand which she has in mind.
P. It gets in your eyes.	
T. Yes it gets in your eyes.	This non-committal reply indicates that while this is true it is not the required answer.
P. It slaps against your face.	
T. It slaps against your face or against your . . . the backs of your legs. That's what I was thinking of . . . It stings . . . If you've been at the seaside and the wind's been blowing the sand blows along and it hurts. And these . . . as these pieces of sand are picked up and blown along like that they rub against one another and they round themselves off and they wear themselves down till they become smaller and smaller and smaller.	None of the replies contains the required idea so the teacher supplies it herself – the abrasive effect of blown sand.

The pupils offer intelligent suggestions but are not able to supply the required idea since it is relevant not merely to what they have been talking about but *to where the teacher intends the lesson to lead.* In such an exchange the pupils can only be dependent upon the teacher's signals: rational thought of their own is unlikely to be rewarded. Such sequences as these are however a normal part of question-and-answer lessons.

My criticism is not that the information is untrue or useless: it is probably helpful to relate the abrasiveness of sand to the children's first-hand experience in this way. It is rather that the question-and-answer method of control must in the long run devalue – in the pupils' eyes as much as in the teacher's – the pupils' capacity for taking a responsible part in learning. Implicitly it devalues both the knowledge they have and their capacity to use speech to apply this knowledge to a new task. (The pupils in the sequence quoted above have no opportunity to use any knowledge, explicit or implicit, which relates to the abrasive action of sand.) From another point of view, such exchanges as these often leave teachers with the sense that their pupils do not know anything useful, and, though they encourage pupils to use the teacher's associations and frames of reference as a model, do not encourage rational problem-solving.

Lessons like the one this is taken from are a normal part of day-to-day schooling in primary and secondary schools. The teacher who taught it would have reason to pride herself on her teaching skills, within the limitations of the question-and-answer pattern of communication. It is the social order which underlies this communication which is open to criticism; as Freire says, such teaching dehumanizes by devaluing and subverting the learner's purposes and sense of reality.

4. Pressures from Outside

If the question-and-answer pattern cannot be accounted for simply as an efficient means to ends which we should all be agreed upon, what are the pressures from outside the classroom which make it so ubiquitous? I cannot pretend to offer more than hints about how this could be answered. In Chapter Five I discussed the teacher's view of knowledge and how this can be related to his own position and hopes. Much of what teachers do can be related to their own position in the school and in the education system generally. An illustration of this can be found in a study of long-stay residential nurseries by Tizard[15] and his associates. The children in the nurseries were between two and five years of age, and were normal or above normal in language development. The investigators were able to show a relationship between the organizational structure of the nurseries and the proportion of the communication between nurses and children which was given to Informative talk as against Control and Supervisory messages. In nurseries where the matron exercised a very rigid control over her nursing staff there was relatively little talk about matters of interest to the children, the kind of talk from which they would be likely to learn. Tizard and his colleagues explained this by suggesting that where nurses were given little autonomy they became primarily concerned with keeping order amongst their charges, at the expense of normal conversation. Whereas when a nurse felt herself to have full responsibility for her charges, she tended to talk with them instead of using language only to control them. Although there are tempting analogies here with what goes on with older children in lessons, it is necessary to remember that nursery nurses would not necessarily see themselves as teaching the children, so a direct comparison with schools might be misleading. Nevertheless, this indicates one process by which the administrative order of a school might influence the communicative order of the classrooms, and thereby influence the curriculum.

Friedenberg[16] made a related point with acid sharpness. He described a large American high school where no pupil could go into the corridors during a lesson without a signed pass, where the main halls were patrolled by police invited to do so by the principal, and where students were supervised even in the lavatories. Friedenberg was horrified most of all by the students' acquiescence in this; what were these students learning about American life and their place in it? 'What is learned in high school', he wrote, 'depends far less on what is taught than on

15. Tizard, B., *et al.* (1972), 'Environmental Effects on Language Development: A Study of Young Children in Long-Stay Residential Nurseries', *Child Development* 43:2, pp. 337–58.

16. Friedenberg, Edgar Z. (1965), *The Dignity of Youth and Other Atavisms*, Boston: The Beacon Press.

what one actually experiences in the place.' No amount of discussion of democracy in history or social studies could erase what these students were learning at first hand – that they were unimportant recipients of a system controlled elsewhere.

We cannot understand how language is used for learning without considering the normative order of the school. This includes both how the school is organized, and the values which are implicitly celebrated in the day-to-day interaction of teachers and pupils. Communication is the common term which links the social order of the school with the curriculum – what the pupils in fact learn. In one sense the social order *is* the pattern of communication. If one asks what it is that constitutes the social order of a school, the answer must refer to (amongst other things) such matters as how teachers and pupils talk to one another in corridors as well as classrooms, how the headmaster runs staff meetings, how timetable decisions are arrived at, and the tone of letters to parents and notices on noticeboards.

An analysis of the social order of a school could not end here but would have to go beyond the school to ask questions about political and economic power. This might include questions about how resources and pupils were channelled to the school and allocated within it, about the pressures bearing upon the headmaster, about the teachers and where they look for professional support and advancement, about the power of the local education authority and of the Department of Education and Science, and about the demands of examinations. A discussion of communication must lead us to consider how knowledge and the social order are related not only inside schools but beyond them in the society of which they are part.[17] Changes inside schools imply concurrent changes outside. But this would take us beyond the scope of this book.

17. Thus Bernstein's discussion of 'classification and framing' offers implicitly to refer not only to school curricula, but to the control of knowledge more widely in the community.

5. Taking Responsibility

A book of this kind almost inevitably ends plaintively, for it is far easier to diagnose ways in which our educational means conflict with our educational ends than to suggest what precisely might be done about this. I have tried to show aspects of classroom communication which are open to change, but have been able to supply no more than hints about what directions the change might take. What I have written will at times have seemed sharply critical of teachers, and I do indeed want to ask teachers to consider whether in their teaching they are doing what they believe they should be doing. I should like to be able to persuade teachers to listen to their pupils more carefully, and also to listen to themselves, sometimes doing both with the aid of a tape-recorder. I should like to hope that the chapter on Transmission and Interpretation will persuade some teachers to ask themselves why they set written work, and how they should respond to it.

Finally, however, what I am wanting to say goes beyond the will of any individual teacher. What I have called communication is not just a matter of the classroom, nor does it involve only teachers and pupils. I might have included (were I qualified to do so) a chapter on how a head teacher can arrange the patterns of communication in his school to see to it that not only the pupils are encouraged to assume wider responsibility, but parents and teachers too. Some head teachers argue persuasively that this is where change in communication must begin. We could go further and consider the communication system between teachers and local authority officials in order to discover why it is that most teachers will attend courses given by authoritative figures but few will take part in self-directed working parties outside the confines of the school. Each communication system is embedded in other larger ones, so that in writing about communication I find myself indulging in vague gestures towards larger things. Yet this is in the nature of social phenomena: in writing about them one is compelled to draw limits, yet at the cost of falsifying. What I have written about is the exercise of power in the classroom, and in writing I have understood afresh the truism that knowledge is power. The question to be asked is how we can make knowledge available to children without making a strait-jacket of it, how we can increase not minimize children's sense that they can take responsibility for their world, and if necessary change it. This is why I have emphasized on the one hand hypothetical and reflexive modes of thought, for they hold the secrets of responsibility and change, and on the other hand the teacher's arbitrary power over classroom knowledge, for it is this that can paralyse children's nascent sense of purpose.

6. Four Disclaimers

In this section I shall make clear what I have *not* been intending, in case any unsympathetic reader is tempted .to use *reductio ad absurdum* as a means of dismissing the case which I have presented.

(1) I have *not* proposed that teachers should never present knowledge to pupils directly. There will always be knowledge to be presented, and established procedures to take pupils through.[18] In recommending an Interpretation viewpoint I am not proposing that children should be left unaided to construct all the knowledge that they need: 'Interpretation' does not mean that. What I am proposing is that patterns of classroom communication should be set up which encourage the formulation of divergent viewpoints, even when from the teacher's point of view these are inadequate. The corollary of this is that pupils should be given time and encouragement to explore the relationship between new knowledge and their existing understanding. This implies less presentation by the teacher and more experiment and interpretation by pupils.

(2) I have *not* recommended the use of small-group discussion as a universal panacea. My purpose has been to urge that pupils

18. Denis Lawton has written: 'One of the functions of a curriculum is to make demands on the children which they would not make on themselves.' *Social Change, Educational Theory and Curriculum Planning*, University of London Press (1973).

should as often as possible be engaged in the formulation of knowledge. For this purpose teachers will naturally use whatever means are appropriate. Although it is true that teacher-class discussion often reduces most pupils to a passive dependence on the teacher, it is not impossible for teachers to change their styles, as the Humanities Curriculum Project team have shown with their 'neutral chairman'. It must always be for the teacher to decide what pattern of communication will engage the pupils' participation, for this must depend not only upon the subject matter which he chooses but also upon his perception of his pupils' willingness to engage with it. No formula can substitute for a teacher's perceptiveness about his pupils' attitude to their work; unfortunately (as we have seen) the planning of subject matter can obscure these perceptions.

(3) I am *not* asserting that all pupils are always ready to take more responsibility for their learning. The extent to which any pupil will work either alone or in a group depends on various factors including whether he finds the subject meaningful. Discussing the differences between the 'latent cultures' from which pupils come, Nell Keddie writes:

It may be that it is ... remoteness from everyday life that is an important element in legitimating academic knowledge in schools. Pupils who have easy access to this knowledge need an ability to sustain uncertainty about the nature of the learning activity in the belief that some pattern will emerge. This requires a willingness to rely on the teacher's authority in delineating what the salient areas of a problem are to be. This will often mean a child putting aside what he 'knows' to be the case in an everyday context.

If this is so, some pupils will undoubtedly find group work threatening since even the teacher's assurance of the meaningfulness of the task has been removed. A possible strategy with such pupils (and they would be predominantly working class if Miss Keddie is right) would be to make explicit the changed interpretation of everyday life which was being presented. For these pupils the ideas put forward here constitute both an opportunity and a threat – an opportunity to explore the relationship of school knowledge to their own lives, but also the threat of being isolated with tasks that will prove alien and meaningless. The teacher's dilemma is how to offer support to these pupils without depriving them of self-respect and self-reliance.

(4) I am *not* recommending that all talk and writing in classrooms should be exploratory. After a lesson in which new ideas have been presented and talked about (and perhaps written about), there is everything to be gained if pupils are asked to stand back from the lesson and ask: What have we been talking about? Which of the things we have said and done are relevant to the main issue and which not? How do they relate to one another? If a teacher asks a class to answer these questions orally, perhaps sorting out replies on the blackboard (or, with older pupils, having them do so), this provides an ideal way of drawing out underlying principles. It would be possible to call this 'final draft' writing, but it would be very different from traditional 'making notes'. My criticism of secondary schools' emphasis on 'final draft' talk and writing is not a criticism of carefully planned, explicit exposition in itself, but a criticism of the practice of expecting such exposition from pupils before they have carried out preliminary explorations.

7. What Underlies Curriculum

There is still much to be done to understand the relation of talking to learning, and the relation of both to the social order set up by teacher and school. Many more studies, both descriptive and experimental, will be needed, so that a book like this can do no more than represent the present state of play as seen through one person's eyes. One purpose of this book is to urge that these questions are part of curriculum, and that any discussion of curriculum innovation which ignores the characteristics of the communication systems in which the new course is to be realized is likely to amount only to shadow-boxing.

What I mean by 'curriculum' is the shaping of understanding, beliefs and values which goes on under the aegis of a school. Undoubtedly teachers' objectives, and their choices of content and method, are important, but they do not by any means consti-tute the whole. The pupils too have 'objectives', beliefs and values which must influence the *effective* curriculum just as much as do the teacher's planned objectives, since the 'shaping of understanding' which I mentioned above is largely their reshaping of existing knowledge. Moreover, every school has organizational and cultural characteristics, so that every teacher brings to the classroom both his version of the school's implicit values, and covert beliefs and assumptions of his own. These implicit goals and beliefs go as far to shape the effective curriculum as do the objectives to which the teacher would give deliberate assent. To understand how these unite to shape the social order of a classroom and thence what children learn, we need the intermediate concept 'communication', which is common both to the public, shared ordering of belief and to the private ordering of belief by individuals. Here a 'psychological' model of learning is not enough: for curriculum theory a social model is needed, for it must acknowledge both learner and social milieu, and include communication from pupil to teacher as well as vice versa.

From a practical point of view too, no amount of central curriculum planning, new materials from Schools Council projects, or exhortations to teachers will make significant changes in what is learnt, if school communication systems remain unchanged. We can apply the idea of reflexivity to teachers too: real change (as opposed to what has been called 'innovation without change') depends on teachers being able and willing to monitor what goes on in their classrooms, in order to match what they see against their own best values. A culture which reduces pupils to passive receivers of knowledge is likely to reduce teachers to passive receivers of curricula, and to deny them the time and resources that would enable them to take active responsibility. Thus an Interpretation view of school learning properly implies an Interpretation view of in-service education for teachers; this means an emphasis not upon packages and ready-made answers, but upon devising ways of encouraging teachers to solve their own problems, and of supporting them in this.

While writing this book I have from time to time been conscious of sounding too classroom-centred, of ignoring how the social order of the classroom responds to outside pressures, social, economic, and cultural. (Consider, for example, how the examination system militates against the hypothetical mode of learning.) This focus upon the classroom has been necessary in order to concentrate attention upon how communication and curriculum – the social order and the cultural order – relate to one another *in that context*. Yet this undoubtedly distorts the view which I have presented. The major educational issue of our time is our failure to achieve an education which is equally available to members of the various sub-cultures which constitute our society. The learner's participation in the control of knowledge is clearly central to this larger educational matter. It would be unrealistic to expect inter-class and inter-ethnic inequalities to be solved in schools when they are so deep-rooted in economic and political inequalities, but this does not absolve teachers from the responsibility for action.

It is not easy to conceive of a classroom in which knowledge is equally accessible to all pupils whatever sub-culture they come from. Such a multi-cultural classroom would accept as meaningful a far wider range of beliefs, understandings and values than any which I have myself observed – or for that matter taught in – so that a facile proposal for multi-cultural classrooms must make demands upon teachers which it is hard to imagine. Certain forms of knowledge lead to future economic and political power; others do not. This underlies the teacher's dilemma which I discussed earlier in this chapter. A multi-cultural classroom, as far as I can imagine it, would be not unlike this:

Inasmuch as the ... range of alternatives of role in different social situations is wide, then individual choices can be made and offered ... Judgments, their bases and consequences, would form a marked content of the communications ... The role system would be continuously accommodating and assimilating the different intents of its members. Looked at from another point of view, the children would be socializing the [teachers] as much as the [teachers] were socializing the children.[19]

But when Bernstein wrote these sentences he was referring not to a classroom but to the open communication system of a

19. Adapted from Bernstein, B. (1971), 'A Socio-linguistic Approach to Socialisation', in *Class Codes and Control*, Vol. 1, Routledge & Kegan Paul.

person-oriented family, and the bracketed word in the last sentence was 'parents' where I have substituted 'teachers'.

If that is the goal, it seems far away when we consider schools as they are, and in particular the way in which primary and secondary schools alike function as selectors of children for future jobs and life-styles. I believe that some of these constraints can and should be resisted, but this will require radical changes in the organization of schooling. It seems most appropriate to end this book by quoting from an American educationist a passage in which he points the relationship between socio-political issues and children's participation in learning.

In our circumstances today we are gradually coming to see that the central problem is social and political: specifically what Bruner calls 'the dispossession of the children of the poor and the alienation of the middle-class child'. And with him we are learning that here too in some sense the medium is the message: it is the school that we must look to, not the curriculum; and beyond the school there is society itself . . . As Bruner says, our first concern must be the mechanisms in the school by which we deprive children of initiative, of a sense of their own value and potency, of their natural, self-determined desire to learn. Those mechanisms are our speciality, and we need to learn how we turn children learning into pupils and students, how we turn ourselves from men teaching into teachers. When we know those answers, then and only then will it be useful for us to take up curriculum as an issue.[20]

20. Douglas, W. W. (1972), 'An American View of the Failure of Curriculum Reform and the Way Ahead', in *English in Education* 6:2, Summer 1972.

Appendix
Setting Up Small Groups

My main thesis in this book is that the learner should take more part in the formulation of knowledge. If this is accepted then the small group clearly offers a way of distancing the teacher's control. But many teachers say that small groups are not a viable way of working for their pupils. They would waste time by talking about something other than the given task, or when they did address themselves to the task they would merely confirm their existing views rather than work to modify them. Yet some teachers do use group methods; indeed the exigencies of equipment and laboratory space force group methods on most secondary school science teachers, though one suspects that many of them have never asked themselves how their pupils are using language while carrying out the tasks. My contention is that they will achieve better learning if they plan for uses of language that will contribute to learning. In Chapter Two, I tried to identify strategies which would contribute to learning: in this appendix, I shall consider how teachers can plan their group work so as to encourage these strategies. The ways in which teachers can influence group work even when they are not present will be considered under five headings:

> a – Feeling of competence
> b – Common ground
> c – Focusing
> d – Pace
> e – Making public

a. *Feeling of Competence*

The most successful discussions amongst those presented in Chapter Two were those in which pupils made an open and collaborative approach. While this is partly governed by personality and by relationships within the group, we all know from introspection that how we take part in a group's activities depends to a considerable degree on how we think our contributions will be valued. If the teacher-class dialogue is strongly shaped by the teacher's sense of relevance, this will affect the pupils' sense of competence in the subject, and probably their approach to small-group work. Uncertainty about 'what teacher wants' is likely to lead to the pursuit of consensus, and to a generally closed approach to learning tasks. The pupils are likely to guess at what the teacher wants instead of trying to make sense of the subject-matter. A first requirement for successful group work is that teachers, whenever they talk to pupils – individually, in groups or in full class – should show that they value their pupils' contributions. This does not mean accepting everything, but it does mean that every teacher should accept that part of his task is to *educate his pupils' sense of relevance* by encouraging them to make connections between new knowledge and old.

Another form of over-insistence on the teacher's goals occurs when pupils are expected to adopt the style of a subject's language at too early a stage. Once again the goals are being over-emphasized at the expense of the pupils' journey towards them. This, too, is likely to damage pupils' feelings of competence. Separating pupils from the language they use every day may be another way of separating them from their everyday knowledge, and depriving them of a sense of competence. New terms should be introduced gradually, and there should be plenty of exploratory discussion and writing without special stylistic demands. If teachers insist too soon on the so-called 'language of the subject' they face the pupils with two tasks at once, organizing thought and guessing what language is acceptable. Some able children can do this easily, but for others this demand is the death of exploratory language, in speech or writing. Learning to play teacher's word-game may be necessary to future specialists, but for most children it is only an extra barrier, for the word is no use to them until they have some grasp of the concept which the word represents.

b. *Common Ground*

In all three of the tasks in Chapter Two the pupils had materials before them. It is essential to this kind of learning that pupils can set up hypothetical ways of organizing or explaining whatever has been put before them, and then return to the materials to see whether the hypotheses do help in dealing with the task, or whether they fail to account for something. Piaget's theories make one expect that children in the later stages of concrete operations will more readily make a leap towards complex and abstract kinds of thinking from a basis of visible and manipulable evidence. It was more surprising to find that all groups used the poem in a similar way.

The point being made is that if pupils are to participate actively in learning it is essential that the evidence on which their suggestions are to be based should be publicly available to them and to some extent under their control. (How one makes public the criteria by which they should determine how they are getting on with the task is a more difficult question.) Work can be based on apparatus, on pictures, on films, or on written materials, or it can be based on shared experience in or outside school. The task for the pupils is essentially to re-interpret experience by recoding it to one another and themselves: this will be impeded if the teacher leans too heavily over them in playing some of his roles – as provider of information or of criteria by which success or failure can be assessed. There is a delicacy to be observed in these parts of a teacher's work: if we overstep the mark, the children may merely learn to imitate, and not benefit from the knowledge we can offer by making it their own.

c. *Focusing*

Education is not a matter of throwing pupils into life at the deep end. We select areas of experience for our pupils, and try to help them to make sense of them. It is perfectly possible to experience air and never stumble across the idea of 'air pressure', which is a construction which men have put upon the way certain things behave. But it is all too easy to try to do the learning for our pupils, to try to by-pass the struggle to recode by dictating the adult version ready-made. If we focus the task too little, the children see no shape in what is before them, and do not know what to do with it, as witness those occasions when children, asked to compile an unstructured 'project', do so merely by copying extracts from books. If we focus too much, we interpose ourselves between the children and the experience we want our pupils to recode; all they can do then is to imitate us.

'Focus' as it is used here is a dual idea. It includes important parts of every teacher's responsibility in directing his pupils' attention: in this respect all three of the tasks set to the groups had been carefully chosen. It is necessary however to emphasize another aspect of focusing, and that is the part that pupils themselves can play. It has already been pointed out that one aspect of successful group work was that pupils were themselves asking questions, in some cases valuable questions, which had not been foreseen by the teacher. Now this too is a form of focusing, and all the more powerful as a means of learning in that it has been set up by the children themselves in a leap of imagination. This raises the question whether children could be deliberately encouraged to learn to ask questions; older pupils might even learn to be connoisseurs of productive questions. In a study published some years ago an American psychologist, Richard Suchman,[1] reported some success in improving the quality of primary school-children's questions.

d. *Pace*

'Pace' is an aspect of the teacher's demands on the class and it is linked with the way critical standards are being applied. If a teacher is hypercritical and insists on every statement being well-shaped and every piece of writing well-organized, the use of language for exploration is ruled out. That is, if the teacher thinks of pupils' language in terms of *performance* instead of in terms of

1. Suchman, J. R., 'The Child and the Inquiry Process', in A. H. Passow (ed.) (1964), *Intellectual Development: Another Look*, Association for Supervision and Curriculum Development.

learning, he will not give them time for the reorganization of thought to take place. And where aspects of pupils' value-systems, of their feelings and attitudes, are involved, as often in the humanities and arts, this is all the more important. You will remember that Group II gained greatly from returning again and again to certain questions. Far from wishing to prevent this by hustling them along, we should be trying to devise methods of persuading other groups to do the same.

Of course, every teacher knows that it is equally unhelpful never to set deadlines to children, or never to demand a finished piece of work. Once again, what is required is a delicate balance between the two. The questions of setting up public standards for pupils to measure their work against, brings us, however, to the last of the five sub-headings.

e. *Making Public*

Although I have stressed the part played in learning by the need to explain our meaning to other people, and therefore to see things from their point of view as well as our own, it would be a mistake to suggest that the effect of an audience is always the same. There is all the difference in the world between working with a few intimate friends to sort out some ideas and making these ideas public to a larger audience. It is not only that some of them may be unsympathetic or even antagonistic; the very size of a group of thirty or so makes a close relationship impossible. Without a close relationship one cannot be sure of shared assumptions, or whether what one says is earning acceptance and agreement. When older children are required to explain something in full class this is a challenge to them to foresee the extra information which they may need to give, and to order their thoughts in an even more explicit and 'public' way. Some cannot accept this challenge, and either keep silent or fail to adjust what they say to the larger group – partly from inability to imagine what needs to be said and partly no doubt from the anxiety resulting from social isolation.

There seems to be every reason to utilize this public demand as a means of urging pupils to organize their thoughts. A teacher is not the ideal audience: the fact that he knows the answer already tends to discourage explicitness, as we saw when the groups reported back to the history teacher. It is not enough merely to place pupils in a public position; first, they need plenty of opportunity to come to terms with their material, to explore the possible ways of saying things without having to pay too heavily for blunders. After that they will need some help in understanding the demands of a more public situation, to understand that they are no longer talking only to the teacher who already knows, but that they must communicate to classmates who may have hardly begun to think about the topic, or even to more distant audiences. This demand can become an instrument of learning.

The effect of an audience is not always the same, in that small-group discussion requires far less *conscious* awareness of other people's needs than does adequate communication with a larger group. I have suggested on page 109 the likely effect of this upon the uses made of language, though at the expense of crudely dichotomizing the two. The small group encourages exploration. Incompleteness and changes of direction, a fairly low level of explicitness, hesitation and lack of an overall plan do not seem out of place amongst intimates who are trying to sort out a complex topic. The same behaviour would be intolerable in a larger group, which would demand explicitness, a more complete organization of thought, and some confidence in phrasing. It might be asked how pupils are to be helped to reach this high level. A partial answer to this is that such clarity and sense of direction depends upon having had *plentiful opportunity to sort out the material first*. This sorting out can well go on in small groups, as we have seen from our four, so long as these preliminary discussions are carefully planned. Classroom learning requires *a full range of uses of language*, from language for exploration at one extreme and language for a strange audience at the other. The former emphasizes the ordering of knowledge for oneself and the latter emphasizes the ordering of knowledge for others. (One might make a similar plea for a range of kinds of writing from the exploratory to the public.) I would go further than this and suggest that exploratory and public uses have a particularly significant interrelation in classroom learning. That is, if they are used together each strengthens the other. Exploratory talk at best enables pupils to reactivate passive knowledge and bring it to bear on a new task, to find their way about a problem and identify its contours or to set up hypotheses and plan techniques. Now there could be no better prepaiation than this for a more public discussion of the same topic, since everyone would be ready to participate, having already brought relevant information to mind and paitly shaped it. Thus, exploratory talk can be seen as a *preparation* for *public* discussion.

On the other hand, as we have seen in our four groups, exploratory discussion can be so closed and unadventurous that the central problems of the topic are avoided rathei than articulated. Here the public discussion may help. If, after time has been given to exploratory discussion, groups are told that they will be presenting their conclusions to the larger group, this has a marked effect on their discussion, which becomes turned increasingly towards the needs of others. Thus, it is possible to use the device of 'reporting back' (in some form or other) to project forward into group discussion new demands for explicitness and orgcniz-ation. But it is important in doing so not to swamp the sense of freedom that lies in ease of relationships and available time, and thus lose the first purely exploratory stage. As a simple model we might consider a sequence like the following.

1. *Focusing Stage* Topic presented in full class. Teacher focuses upon the topic, encourages pupils to verbalize necessary preliminary knowledge, and if appropriate makes a demonstration to form the basis for group work.

2. *Exploratory Stage* Pupils carry out any necessary manipulations of materials, and talk about issues which their attention has been directed towards.

3. *Reorganizing Stage* Teacher refocuses attention, and tells groups how they will be reporting back, and how long they have to prepare for it.

4. *Public Stage* Groups present their findings to one another and this leads to further discussion.

No doubt this sequence is both idealized and very familiar. What is new here is the emphasis on the changing functions of language in the course of the sequence, and especially upon the mutual reinforcing of the last two stages.

Perhaps it should be pointed out that 'reporting back' is being used here in a very general way. There are many possibilities, including the display of work done by groups in written form, by distributing duplicated copies or by a wall-display. It might even be argued that this more permanent written form should be seen as a fifth stage to follow the public discussion.

Teachers who read this for practical advice on managing group work will by now be demanding an example. In Chapter Two I gave some real examples; here is one constructed to illustrate how group work can fit into an ongoing teaching sequence. A teacher with a class of eleven-year-olds in a middle school is responsible for a loosely defined area of study called 'Environmental Studies', which he takes to include both physical and social phenomena. During lessons related to the general topic of 'Pollution' some pupils have talked about purifying things, and it has become clear that the children could usefully study both the physical distinction 'pure/impure' and the social issues raised by 'clean/dirty'.

The teacher decides to make his first approach to this via the familiar purifying of rocksalt (see Nuffield *Combined Science 11–13*, Section 1:7), and introduces into the next lesson various 'dirty' objects including rocksalt.

After presenting the idea of dirt and cleansing to the class, he puts them into groups to discuss how the various materials might be cleaned. Some of the materials generate simple answers, but not the rocksalt. He leaves the groups to talk for no more than ten minutes before calling them together for class discussion; the group discussion had been primarily intended for exploratory purposes in order to make pupils' existing understandings more available to reflection.

A class discussion follows, based on issues raised in the groups; the teacher eventually focuses the attention of the class upon the rocksalt and the concept 'pure/impure'. He elicits from his pupils a range of suggestions about how salt can be purified, sees that each group has chosen a method, and makes appropriate apparatus available. As he goes round the working groups he leaves with them questions to be considered: 'What happens when you filter? Where is the salt now? What's the point of heating it?' and so on.

During the practical work his conversations with pupils have helped him to identify the conceptual difficulties facing his pupils, and this enables him, as the practical work draws to a close, to write a series of questions on the blackboard. 'You've done your experiment,' he says. 'Now you've got to sort out what happened.' At this point the pupils turn their attention from manipulating apparatus to collaborating (in the same groups) in making sense of what they did and observed. When he sees that most of the groups have taken the discussion as far as they can on their own, he brings the class together again, and asks all of the groups to present their conclusions and to discuss one another's. These interpretative discussions, first in groups and then all together, he sees as the most important part of the lesson.

Next he may move towards distilling water, or towards the social issues raised by the concept of 'dirt'. This latter topic might begin in groups by asking the pupils to talk about: 'What do your mothers mean by "getting dirty"? When are they worried about it? When aren't they? Why does it matter? Does dirt harm anyone?' These questions will tap a whole range of first-hand experience and start the pupils looking at it afresh. Moreover it will prepare for a class discussion in which he can move them towards seeing the arbitrariness of the concept of dirt, and possibly prepare for some work in categorizing things. Later they will write about methods of purifying things, or about our dislike of things which we call dirty.

Every experienced teacher who reads the foregoing paragraphs will recognize that this account is highly idealized. Some will say that this approach would be too time-consuming, though others might think the time well-spent. (Teachers' ideas about 'covering ground' and 'shortage of time' would make an interesting study: one might ask where they come from, and what view of knowledge they imply.) My intention here has been merely to show that group discussion can be planned within existing patterns of work, and that it can contribute valuably to the general exploration of a new topic and to a more focused discussion based on questions prepared by a teacher. Group talk of this kind both strengthens class discussion and (at best) supports forms of learning which take place less readily in full class.

Afterword

A small study group of preservice and inservice teachers, graduate students, and university faculty met during the 1990–1991 school year to discuss *From Communication to Curriculum*. Our goal was to explore the role of "talk" in small-group discussions of shared texts. Through participation in our group discussions we hoped to rethink the relationship between literature discussions and the larger curriculum, to develop ways of listening to the talk in these literature discussions that would enable us to understand the meanings and connections our learners were constructing, and to support more effectively the learning of all students engaged in these small-group experiences. In order to do this, we agreed to read *From Communication to Curriculum,* and other writings by Douglas Barnes, to make and analyze tapes of literature discussion groups in our various classrooms (or existing dissertation data), and to read and share related professional materials, with several of us volunteering to make informal presentations.

While we are still sorting through the topics we addressed in relation to this book, we feel we can offer two insights of interest to others. First, this powerful text invites subsequent generations of educators to return to it again and again and find new and productive ways of viewing current issues. Our experience as a study group has convinced us that this book, first published in 1976 and repeatedly reprinted since that time, has the potential for stimulating discussions about issues we face in classrooms today. The second point is that experience in a small, collaborative inquiry group has informed our understanding of the reading process, the social nature of learning, the power of small-group experiences, and the need to engage in exploratory talk as a part of the learning process. Our new understandings help us to be better learners and, perhaps more importantly, to help our students to be better learners.

What Did We Talk About?

Our initial discussions focused on two major areas: 1) getting acquainted in order to build a collaborative learning group, and 2) identifying initial topics and questions from our reading of the text, which we discussed with others. We described our teaching situations, history with literature discussion groups, professional connections with other members of the group, and reasons for wanting to read and discuss this book with others. We were invited to join the group because each of us added a unique perspective to the discussions. One group member served as a resource for related professional literature while another brought extensive experiences in analyzing audio-tapes of small-group talk. The classroom teachers enriched our discussions with real understanding of the critical issues facing schools, while the preservice teachers helped to make the familiar unfamiliar through their insightful questions and challenges to our assumptions about the way things had to be in schools. Most of us were already familiar with the book and were making the choice to reread the text with the support of a professional literature discussion group.

The initial list of topics and questions for discussion, developed in small groups, provided the starting point for subsequent discussions. The initial list included:

1. How can we encourage and support collaborative small-group experiences when they are an unfamiliar format for instruction?
2. How does Barnes define curriculum, and what are the classroom implications of this definition?
3. What do we learn about the social nature of the classroom by exploring the hidden curriculum?
4. How are Barnes's notions of exploratory and presentational talk related to our classrooms?

Subsequent discussions extended these questions in relationship to our classroom experiences. Each session included time to discuss and debate aspects of the book as well as share current concerns and recent classroom experiences. The following summarizes three of the major themes in our conversations across one school year. We offer our experiences not as a template for the discussions of others, but as an example of the potential Barnes has created for teachers to view their classrooms in ways which promote needed change.

   1. Barnes values the role of talk in the classroom as both a vehicle for learning and as a rich source of data for analyzing and evaluating classroom experiences. When language is viewed as a vehicle for learning rather than a content subject to be learned for its own sake, teachers are encouraged to focus on using language to understand students: the unique perspectives they bring to classroom experiences, the ways they are using language to make sense of new experiences, and what they are learning. These insights enabled us to develop more effective means of observing and evaluating the literature discussions in our classrooms.

   Our interest in talk led us to make connections to the work of other language researchers to help us understand social and class differences in talk, the functions language serves in various situations, and language learning in various settings. We also considered the power of language for building community, for expressing and transmitting culture, and for empowering learners — particularly as we struggled to understand the role of language and literacy in the lives of our own students. These discussions rekindled our commitment to building a supportive *social* community in our classrooms as a necessary prerequisite to developing a successful *learning* community.

   2. Barnes focuses his attention on curriculum as embedded in the social life and conversation of the classroom. This view of curriculum led us to make frequent connections to the work of Louise Rosenblatt, specifically *The Reader, The Text, The Poem* (Carbondale, IL: Southern Illinois University Press, 1978). Rosenblatt had interest in reading not on the reader or the text, but on the "poem" created by the transaction between reader and text. In discussing Barnes' views of curriculum in relationship to Rosenblatt's notion of the reading experience, we described curriculum as the transaction between the learner and the classroom experience, a transaction that results in a shared, yet unique,"poem" for each participant.

   Applying these ideas to literature discussion groups encouraged us to see the talk that occurred in these groups as windows on the meanings our readers were constructing through their transactions with the text and with one another. Further, we began to relate the role of these literature discussions more effectively to the ongoing reading and learning experiences of the classroom. Our attention to the social nature of learning encouraged us to consider how teachers plan meaningful social experiences in the classroom: establishing a collaborative learning environment, supporting groups of learners in using language and other communication systems to explore and construct meanings, and understanding role relationships as they affect the functioning of groups.

3. Barnes distinguishes between exploratory and presentational talk, arguing that the most effective small-group discussions are those in which participants explore and construct new meanings. This distinction led us to analyze the ways in which our learners, and we, were using talk to explore new meanings of shared text and the ways in which teachers support and inhibit such conversations in the classroom. Before such effective talking to learn can occur, the classroom climate must be a safe learning environment in which learners are encouraged to function in a research community. Second, small group work often encourages exploratory talk, particularly when the teacher encourages learners to assume responsibility for the discussion.

Barnes describes exploratory talk in small groups as that in which participants use language to move the group along to new understandings. As our study group grappled with this concept, we recognized and came to value our own use of exploratory talk. We offered tentative ideas, argued and debated with one another in a comfortable exchange, and cited examples from the text to support and clarify points. At the same time, recognizing our use of exploratory talk in our small-group learning helped us identify examples of exploratory talk in our tapes of small-group discussions. Further, we began to appreciate the analysis of such talk as providing insights into the meanings our learners were constructing. Understanding the role this talk played in our learning helped us see the potential for talking to learn in our classrooms. This led us to discussion of the teacher's responsibility in supporting successful small-group discussions. The debate over teacher-directed versus student-directed discussions was recast as one of defining the collaborative relationship between teachers and their students in negotiating curriculum.

How Did We Function as a Study Group?

Members of our study group acknowledged one common reason for joining: we were seeking discussion with a professionally stimulating group, thereby expanding our understanding of the potential of small-group learning experiences and curriculum. Like the TAWL (Teachers Applying Whole Language) support groups, that have emerged across the United States, Canada, and Australia, we wanted a support group for our own learning.

All of us had participated in teacher support groups, other professional meetings, and, most importantly, literature discussion groups with our own students. This study group experience was unique, however, requiring that we sort out our new roles and responsibilities, interests, and course of action. In so doing we often drew upon our classroom experiences with students for guidance. This comparison between *our* "Barnes study group" experiences and our understanding of literature discussion groups, between *our* learning and the structure of a classroom curriculum, proved to be a powerful heuristic device. The insights from one perspective informed and challenged the other perspective.

In addition to our discussions of the text, we began to analyze the tapes we had made of small group discussions. The questions that guided our analyses were influenced by both our prior experiences with literature discussion groups and our responses to the text. The questions included four major areas: 1) the nature and content of the talk of learners in a literature discussion group with or without a teacher present or participating; 2) the talk of learners as a vehicle for evaluating and sharing learners' growth as readers; 3) the talk of learners as it varies by race or gender and from one group discussion to another; and 4) the role and responsibility of the teacher in supporting or inhibiting productive discussions.

As we further developed and refined our agenda and social roles within the group, we consulted others for guidance. We chose these outside resource persons because they were familiar with literature discussion groups, with teacher support groups such as TAWL, and with the work of Barnes. Dorothy and Douglas Barnes influenced the actions of our group through their correspondence with us, their professional writings, and their presentations and conversations with us in St. Louis.

What Are the New Questions We Are Asking?

Having learned some new ways of analyzing the talk in literature discussion groups and ways of considering curriculum, we found that we had returned to questions many of us had asked shortly after venturing into literature discussion groups in our classrooms:

1. What do we value in a literature discussion?
2. What characteristics signal a successful discussion group experience?
3. How do we define growth or progress in our learner's encounters with text?

Similarly, as we reflected on our own experiences as members of a collaborative learning group, we returned to earlier questions about the nature of learning, the role of language in the learning process, the social organization of classrooms (and schools), and the needs and intentions of our learners.

While we had asked and tentatively answered these questions before, we returned to them with our new insights. Thus, we found we are now actually involved in answering new questions because we, and the potential represented in the questions, have been changed through our experiences. An example of Rosenblatt's reader-text transaction, our exploratory talk with others changed the way we view these questions. We are no longer satisfied with our earlier answers to these questions because we have been changed through our transaction with this text, and with one another.

The realization that returning to old questions initiates an inquiry in a new direction was difficult for us to accept.

Members of the study group experienced a sense of frustration as we struggled with conflicting feelings. We were torn between the need to celebrate what we had accomplished, and the need to confront these new questions. Just when we thought we were understanding literature discussion groups, somebody would ask a question that reminded us that there is so much more to know about them. We realize even more the need to focus our attention on understanding and valuing the needs and language of our increasingly diverse groups of students.

As we reflect on our year as a study group, we recognize that participation in a small-group, collaborative inquiry has been a significant one for us. At different times we have speculated on the future of the group, commenting on how much we have come to depend on the group for support, encouragement, insight, and professional challenge. We have questioned whether anyone else could ever truly feel a member of the group without having this shared history. These reflections became more powerful as we considered the implications for learners in our classrooms. We returned once again to Barnes as he helps us shift our perspective "from communication to curriculum."

Although this book was originally published in 1976, we found much to stimulate and enlighten our discussions of contemporary educational issues in the 1990s. We benefited tremendously from seeing classrooms through the lens provided by Barnes. We feel our students have benefited indirectly as a result of the changes in our thinking and actions relative to curriculum.

We believe our experience serves as one example of what Barnes might accept as a successful curricular experience. We came together from unique backgrounds but with a shared interest; we read, discussed, disagreed, argued, explored, and created new meanings and presented well-worked ideas to others . Using connections we made between his text and our life experiences, we used the support of the group to work at understanding our teaching, our students, and the power of talk in the learning experience.

We invite others to form or join small professional study groups — within TAWL groups or schools or by telephone across distances — to read, reread, and discuss this and other professional texts that have the potential to encourage meaningful change in teaching and learning.

Kathryn Mitchell Pierce

St. Louis, Missouri, June 1991

Index of Names